Decoding Culture

Decoding Culture

Theory and Method in Cultural Studies

Andrew Tudor

SAGE Publications
London • Thousand Oaks • New Delhi

#4274609S

© Andrew Tudor 1999

First published 1999

SAGE Publications Ltd
6 Bonhill Street
London EC2A 4PU

SAGE Publications Inc
2455 Teller Road
Thousand Oaks, California 91320

SAGE Publications India Pvt Ltd
32, M-Block Market
Greater Kailash – I
New Delhi 110 048

British Library Cataloguing in Publication data

A catalogue record for this book is
available from the British Library

ISBN 0 7619 5246 2
ISBN 0 7619 5247 0 (pbk)

Library of Congress catalog record available

Typeset by M Rules
Printed in Great Britain by Biddles Ltd, Guildford, Surrey

Contents

1 *The Story So Far*

Some time in 1963, then a sociology undergraduate of strongly held opinions but little knowledge, I was moved to hurl Richard Hoggart's *The Uses of Literacy* across the room and out through my open bedsit window. So absolute was his condemnation of 'Juke-Box boys' and the rest of the burgeoning post-war youth culture that I took his book as a gross calumny visited upon what appeared to me to be the most exciting set of cultural changes since the emergence of the cinema. My anger was made all the more self-righteous by the nostalgia that cloaked his account of the working-class culture of his youth (I fancied myself a hard-headed Leninist at the time, and had little truck with such romanticism) and his evident belief in the superiority of that older culture over the new. By a nice irony I could just about see from my window the area of Leeds of which he had written, and as I sheepishly rescued the book from the dirty puddle into which it had fallen, the sight of those rows of decaying back-to-backs should have been more than enough to teach me a lesson about the perils of youthful arrogance and the many forms that understanding can take.

Needless to say it did no such thing, and I returned to my reading of Hoggart in a mood of determined dissent combined with sociological evangelism. I had no way of knowing then, of course, that in terms of previous critical discussions Hoggart's book was actually a significant move in my direction, for all its antagonism to the popular culture that so fascinated me. Nor did I suspect that both the author and his book would play a vital role in initiating the field of 'cultural studies' and that much of my subsequent academic life would be caught up in the ramifications of that innovation. Had I known, I would probably have been horrified at the thought of such inter-disciplinary miscegenation, let alone at the prospect of playing any part in it. These were crusading years in British sociology, and mine and my contemporaries' commitment to our embattled discipline was deeply felt.

By the time I graduated I was rather less puritan in my beliefs, and when I first met Hoggart in 1965 – he gave me a peripatetic job interview which began, somewhat unusually, with an appointment outside the main entrance of a well known Leeds department store – I was no longer of a mind to cast him or his ideas out of the window. As far as I recall (and this is not reliable since the 'interview' involved a pint or two of Tetley's mild) I never even confessed to my earlier indiscretions with his book. Nor, however, did I go to work at the newly created Birmingham Centre for Contemporary Cultural Studies of which Hoggart was the founding Director. Had I done so, perhaps my relationship to the next 30 years of cultural studies history would have been quite different. Certainly I would have experienced it much more from within, compared to the rather sceptical and somewhat distanced position that I have maintained over the subsequent decades.

I tell this story less in a nostalgic frame of mind than with the aim of giving my reader some sense of the background from which this book emerges – where I am coming from, to borrow an ugly but apposite phrase. Indeed, shorn of its youthful exuberance, my ballistic response to *The Uses of Literacy* could stand as a microcosm of my attitude to cultural studies more generally. An uneasy and ambiguous combination of fascination with its subject matter, impatience with at least some aspects of its more 'literary critical' inheritance, fury with its tendency toward exclusivism and theoretical fashion, admiration for its inter-disciplinary inventiveness, and sympathy with its politically critical project. For over 30 years I have watched the monster grow, largely as an interested observer, though sometimes – especially where my first love, the cinema, was concerned – as a more active participant. It has been an eventful history. I have seen the rise and fall of several marxisms, battles fought for possession of the true structuralist spirit, disciplinary boundaries crumble then rebuild themselves, psychoanalytic concepts of unparalleled obscurity spread far and wide, active readers emerge to be celebrated, and passive victims of media manipulation laid to uneasy rest.

Throughout this time I have been puzzled. Where did it all come from, this intense commitment to remaking the map of culture, and why did it take the form that it did? How was it that scholars trained in disciplines normally consumed by mutual disrespect, not to mention hatred, came to co-operate across the newly encountered terrain? What intellectual earthquake gave rise to the extraordinary fascination with theory (or perhaps it should be 'Theory') that pervaded academic pursuits not previously distinguished by their engagement with systematic abstraction? Along what road had we travelled such that an abiding desire to discriminate between high and low, good and bad culture, was transmuted into a body of thought directed at analytic understanding but with no particular reference to the aesthetic or moral value of specific artefacts? In short, what is cultural studies, where did it come from, and what are its logics?

What cultural studies is not

In some part, this book is my answer to these questions. It is not a complete answer, nor could it be. I make no claim to be defining 'cultural studies' here or to be defending some such paradigmatic practice. What I shall try to do is lay out the kinds of arguments that formed what Chaney (1994: 9) wisely prefers to call 'the *field* of cultural studies' in full recognition that there is much more to which the label attaches than I shall consider here. In so doing I shall be examining many of the individual works and schools of thought that feature in the standard textbooks of the area (for example Turner, 1990, or Storey, 1993). However, it is important to stress that I am not seeking to provide an alternative to those excellent introductory texts. My aim here is to present an analytic history of cultural studies that focuses primarily upon the field's theoretical and methodological dynamics. My exposition, therefore, is not designed with a view to the completeness of coverage that a textbook would require; instead I select the analytic issues that I consider to be the most significant. In general terms I shall return constantly to issues of epistemology and ontology. What kind of knowledge claims are made by different cultural studies practices and on what grounds are they warranted? What kinds of assumptions do they make about the nature of culture and social life and what are their implications? And perhaps most generally of all, what conceptions do they hold concerning the ubiquitous tension between the structuring capacity of cultural forms and the activity of human agency?

My aim, then, is analytic, not descriptive. Indeed, even to try to describe everything to which the term cultural studies has been applied would keep us here from now until Doomsday, and later still. Over 20 years ago Colin Sparks (1996a: 14) opened a discussion of cultural studies' evolution by observing how difficult it was to offer any kind of precise definition: '[a] veritable rag-bag of ideas, methods and concerns from literary criticism, sociology, history, media studies, etc., are lumped together under the convenient label of cultural studies'. As many later commentators have, he resolved his definitional problem by attending primarily to the work of the Centre for Contemporary Cultural Studies, a move which is convenient but which has become increasingly misleading as the years have gone by. Sparks is guiltless in this respect; he recognizes that the CCCS' work represents 'a very limited part' of the larger and more complex enterprise. Later authors – not least those who have sought to carry the word of British cultural studies across the Atlantic – have been less scrupulous however, and contemporary students looking to such sources for enlightenment could be forgiven for thinking that the CCCS and 'cultural studies' were more or less conterminous.

That is at one end of the scale. At the other end, the question of definition is dealt with not by restriction but by unfettered inflation. This was always likely, of course, given the range of disciplinary environments on which early cultural studies drew. But even some of the more precise attempts to formulate the parameters of the enterprise have found themselves rapidly ascending the ladder of generality. Richard Johnson's (1986: 45) much quoted 'What is Cultural Studies Anyway?' at one point sees the cultural studies project as being 'to abstract, describe and reconstitute in concrete studies the social forms through which human beings "live", become conscious, sustain themselves subjectively'. Some might claim that to be a decent enough definition of sociology rather than cultural studies, though not Johnson, who writes as a historian and a marxist, and it certainly proclaims a very large field of study. Again, as time has gone by, less rather than more care has been exercised, with the 1990s bringing a vast increase in work labelled 'cultural studies' but sharing little more than that label itself. The seemingly exponential growth of textbooks and edited collections is clearly feeding a hunger for the subject, whatever it might be, but it is also bringing with it a diffuseness which does nothing to improve our sense of what the project is all about.

Of course, I recognize that I too am contributing to this expansion by writing this book. In mitigation I shall immediately concede that I am not seeking to define cultural studies, or limit it to some set of practices that I think are right and proper. I shall use the term rather as people in everyday life use genre categories such as romantic fiction or horror: that is, to invoke a tradition which is presumed to exhibit significant shared features and which would be recognized as such by a culturally competent observer. This does not exclude boundary disputes since, like genres and other disciplines, cultural studies is necessarily blurred at its edges. Indeed, cultural studies is especially so in that it is itself comprised of inputs from a whole range of disciplinary environments that pre-existed it. One of its principal distinguishing characteristics is precisely that it drew together conceptual material which began life in other disciplinary domains but which was transmuted in the transfer from one context to another. Linguistics, literary criticism, media research, sociology, philosophy, history, film studies, and others, are all part of the genetic mix of cultural studies. It is hardly surprising, then, that we should find centrifugal inclinations in such a trans-disciplinary 'discipline'. As Frow (1995: 7) observes, 'cultural studies exists in a state of productive uncertainty about its status as a discipline'.

Since the task of disciplinary definition is fruitless in any form that escapes vacuity, I shall instead try to examine the main analytic positions that have been historically recognized as prominent in the formation of the field. By constructing an analytic history I shall be able to examine the arguments linking various elements in the cultural studies mix, so identifying the key concepts that have

moulded analysis and the key problems that have surfaced repeatedly. Inevitably that results in serious omissions, particularly in
the recent period when cultural studies has spiralled out into a
whole range of new applications. For instance, I shall not discuss
the emergence of 'post-colonial' cultural studies, or the significant
recent considerations of race and 'otherness' in culture. This is
not because I consider these issues unimportant. It is because, for
all their undoubted importance, they are not addressed to the central analytic problems of the cultural studies tradition. Even those
issues associated with the so-called 'postmodern turn' (the decline
of 'grand narratives', relativism, fluid subjectivity, and the like) will
only interest me here in as much as they can be seen to have
emerged, not from the force of postmodernity itself, but as a consequence of the internal logics of the tradition. Postmodern
cultural form is an interesting topic for cultural studies research,
but its ideas are less than interesting as a conceptual resource for
cultural studies theory. This judgement might have to alter, of
course, although views on that will vary according to the degree to
which recent cultural change is seen as a recognisable extension of
late modernity or a more radical dislocation. On that question the
jury is still out, and, while I know my own position, it would be pre-
mature here to speculate upon the likely verdict.

Once upon a time

What, then, is the broad shape of this 'history' that I shall examine?
In the much simplified narrative that will occupy the rest of this
chapter – and structure the rest of the book – I shall view it as a
series of phases, the move from one to the next occasioned by perceived failings of each and consequent attempts to reconstruct the
tradition in such a way as to overcome those failings. Note that this

does not necessarily imply an overall progression. The fact that at each transition specifiable difficulties are addressed does not mean that they are actually resolved. Nor does this dynamic produce a linear process of intellectual evolution, however much it may look like that in the schematic narrative that I shall provide. As the more detailed discussion of later chapters illustrates, the road-map of cultural studies is not without its byways, diversions and motor-way interchanges.

I do believe, however, that there is a key 'moment' in the emergence of cultural studies without which this history would be so markedly different as to constitute quite another intellectual enterprise. This moment reflects the extraordinary impact of structuralism on the nascent field of study. While it is conventional to single out the early contributions of the likes of Richard Hoggart and Raymond Williams as constitutive of the cultural studies project – and I too will consider them in that light in Chapter 2 – the real turning point comes later. In the latter part of the 1960s many disciplines were affected (and affronted) by a body of ideas and analytic methods imported from France. Ultimately rooted in Saussure's structural linguistics, these seemingly arcane ideas were to alter for ever the direction and character of cultural studies. It was structuralism that offered a flag under which an otherwise motley collection of inter-disciplinary mercenaries could unite, however precariously. And it was through the terms of structuralist theories that, at least for a time, diverse inputs could be synthesized into a larger endeavour. There is a real sense in which cultural studies is a child – a bastard child, perhaps – of structuralism.

But I get ahead of myself. To appreciate the magnitude of the impact of structuralism it is first necessary to consider the kinds of views of culture and cultural analysis that preceded its intervention. Aspiring cultural analysts of my generation were faced with a firmly entrenched view of culture. At its foundation was the idea of critical discrimination and the assumption that it was essential to distinguish between high and low culture. On this account, the twentieth century had seen the spread of new and largely undesirable forms of mass culture – cultural artefacts produced in industrial style for the diversion and entertainment of the urban masses. The goal of literary and cultural criticism was to ensure the preservation of quality in the face of this challenge, and to analyse culture, therefore, was to make such informed judgements. Even in sociology, where the question of cultural value was less to the fore, it was widely assumed that mass culture was inferior and required little in the way of sophisticated analysis for its proper understanding. Media research was thus dominated by a concern with the (adverse) effects of popular cultural forms and by the then widely discussed concept of 'mass society'.

For those engaged in higher education in the late 1950s and the first half of the 1960s this established view of culture became increasingly unacceptable, in part because of its insistent elitism, but also because it precluded a coherent and appropriately sensitive analysis of popular culture. The widespread assumption that 'mass culture' was intrinsically crude meant that little or no attention was paid to the everyday culture of most of the population, whether the historic class-based traditions (like that described by Hoggart) or the newly emergent youth cultures of the period. In literary criticism, in educational studies, in the sociology of the media, there was growing dissatisfaction with the inability of the prevailing view of culture to say anything interesting about the new and vibrant popular cultural forms. All that was available was simple condemnation and a somewhat patronizing desire to equip the young with the ability to discriminate.

It was in this context that what might be called 'popular cultural studies' emerged, initially without a clear programme other than to

afford to popular culture the attention that it was presumed to
merit. This move was driven by some of the same considerations
that had formed the terms of traditional cultural analysis, at least in
as much as it evinced a desire to demonstrate the aesthetic and
moral quality of the likes of Hollywood cinema or popular music.
But, influenced also by less art-centred views of culture and by
those, like Williams, who argued that culture should be understood as deeply embedded in the lives of ordinary people, there
was also pressure to examine cultural artefacts and their users in a
more holistic and systematic way. It was in this project that the first
tentative steps toward cross-disciplinary fertilization were seen,
and it was here also that there was growing awareness of the need
for a new framework and method of analysis. By the later years of
the 1960s this search was beginning to focus on the concept of
'language'. Processes of communication, whether in art, film, television or fiction, were clearly language-like in some sense. Perhaps
it would be around the concept of language that a new unity of
approach could be forged.

So it proved, for it was only when attention turned to the theories of language and culture developed in French structuralism
that diffuse resistance to traditional modes of analysis found a positive theoretical focus. As we shall see in Chapter 2, the break with
tradition heralded by Hoggart, Williams and the new analysts of
popular culture was incomplete. It needed the structuralist input to
shift discussion onto a radically different terrain – that of signification. At this point the story becomes much more complicated and
I shall have to skate over details that will be given lengthier consideration later. Minimally it is necessary to distinguish two
successive phases of structuralist influence, the first of which
revolved around the attempt to apply Saussurian ideas to all kinds
of processes of signification, while the second sought to relocate
the resulting over-formal analysis of cultural texts into its historical,

social and psychoanalytic context. Provided not too much weight is attached to the terms themselves, these two phases can usefully be thought of as 'structuralist' and 'post-structuralist' cultural studies.

In the structuralist phase the informing ideas are those found in a series of famous Saussurian concepts. I shall not examine those ideas here; they are given a full discussion in Chapter 3. Their import was to focus attention on the systems of 'language' that enabled communication in diverse cultural forms. If people communicated, the reasoning ran, then that was a consequence of a shared set of codes and conventions upon which they drew. So, whatever the cultural form on which analysis focused – film, television, fiction, photography, or any other communicative mode – the structuralist goal was to uncover the underlying system upon which communication depended. Saussure had envisaged a science of signs to which he had given the name 'semiology'. In this first phase of structuralist cultural studies that semiological ideal loomed large, even if in actuality it was rarely, if ever, achieved.

In analytic practice, as seen in the work of Lévi-Strauss, early Barthes, and a host of enthusiastic borrowers of their ideas, this gave rise to complex analyses of 'texts' of all shapes and sizes. At last cultural analysis had found a new method, and one, furthermore, that transcended disciplinary restrictions in the name of a 'scientific' decoding of the workings of culture. It was also a method that encouraged a dominantly formal approach to the texts under analysis, one in which the operation of the signs that made up a text was all too easily rendered as an emergent product of the significatory system alone. Although the original Saussurian theory viewed language very much in its social context, the first phase of its application to cultural studies rather neglected this social potential in favour of using his concepts in formal textual analysis. Quite quickly, however, exponents of the new method became aware of the problems arising from this formalism, and by the beginning of the 1970s it was clear that 'structuralism' alone was insufficient. Although it had provided a method of analysis appropriate for a cultural studies with ambitions to examine a wide range of forms of culture, that analysis was now in need of theoretical and empirical integration into a larger account of the contexts of communication.

The search for that larger account is reflected here, as it was elsewhere, in the move from 'structuralism' to 'post-structuralism', and it was to generate the basic theoretical terms in which the nascent discipline would come into its own. It is at this point in my narrative that we reach a major parting of the ways in cultural studies. One form of post-structuralism – that associated with the journal *Screen* and referred to here as '*Screen* theory' – would embrace an essentially psychoanalytic approach to the constitution of subjectivity, while a second – developed mainly in the work of the Centre for Contemporary Cultural Studies – would lean on Gramscian theories of hegemony in their analysis of the social and historical role of cultural forms. Both positions saw ideology as a key concept and both laid claim to historical materialism as an informing perspective. But the modes of analysis to which their different post-structuralisms gave rise would develop into two contrasting approaches to cultural studies.

In *Screen* theory (the main focus of Chapter 4) the key ideas were derived from Althusser's theory of ideology and focused upon the capacity of texts and discourses to position 'readers' as particular subjects. By being constituted as a certain kind of subject by cultural materials, an individual was caught within ideology. Accordingly, texts were to be analysed with a view to uncovering these processes of 'interpellation': the ways in which our sense of ourselves as distinctive subjects was constructed through and by the systems of discourse that made up our culture. How best to theorize such processes of subject constitution? For *Screen* theory it became foundational to assume that psychoanalytic concepts would provide privileged access to these processes, notably through terms drawn from the 'structuralist' development of psychoanalytic theory pioneered by Jacques Lacan. Thus, by yoking together a theory of ideology that focused upon the construction of subjects, and a psychoanalytic account of that process itself, *Screen* theory was able, formally at least, to locate structural analysis in a social and psychoanalytic context. From these beginnings there developed the whole tradition of 'subject positioning theory' which, to this day, retains an important role in cultural analysis.

The crucial period for the development of *Screen* theory was during the first half of the 1970s, and by the middle of that decade it had reached its high point of influence. It was very controversial, with critics accusing the theory of over-determinism, of psychoanalytic reductionism, and of betraying *Screen*'s political project by retreating into the obscurantism of Lacanian terminology. Among these critics were members of the *Screen* group itself, as well as those within the CCCS who had made it their business to engage with this particular extension of structuralism. The CCCS had also been much influenced by the first phase of structuralist thinking and, while rejecting *Screen*'s formulation of post-structuralism, was eager to find its own way of carrying things forward. Convinced that ideology was the key concept through which to relate structural analysis of texts to larger political and social dynamics, they too drew upon Althusser. However, rather than extending Althusser's ideas in the ways found in *Screen* theory, they sought increasingly to theorize ideology in terms derived from Gramsci's work.

We will examine this version of post-structuralist cultural studies in some detail in Chapter 5. For the purposes of the present outline it is only necessary to note that the CCCS position, while preserving a central emphasis on ideology, rejected the strongly text-driven model that *Screen* had derived from Althusser and Lacan. For the CCCS, culture was a site of constant conflict, a significatory terrain across which attempts to secure hegemony – in effect, domination by consent of the dominated – were variously resisted. Class remained a key concept. Although it was increasingly recognized that gender and race were important structuring features of social life, in its main period of influence the CCCS was committed to class-based analysis first and foremost. That was in the late 1970s and early 1980s, at which time both the Centre and its then Director, Stuart Hall, produced a remarkable body of work. Hall in particular pushed cultural studies theory forward; and the series of papers that he published during this period are probably the most influential cultural studies writing to come from the pen of a single individual.

In spite of the quality of that work, however, it became apparent in the course of the Thatcherite 1980s that something was amiss with this neo-Gramscian synthesis. Doubts had been growing in the social sciences and humanities about the effectiveness of class-based general theories, and it was also becoming clear that the polysemic potential of culture – its inherent capacity for multiple meanings and ambiguity – was significantly greater than even the CCCS model could encompass. Saussurian structuralism had always recognized that semiotic systems were complex and under-determined, by their very nature open to plural 'readings' – although language systems did indeed set limits on communication processes, they were rarely simple or straightforward enough to do so unambiguously. However, in embedding structuralism in a context that viewed culture as ideology, as a key element in securing hegemony, the CCCS framework was obliged to minimize these polysemic aspects of communication. How else could the dominant ideology be effective? Accordingly, CCCS thinking sought to understand the relationship between cultural texts and readers as one in which the basic reference point was a hegemonic 'preferred reading'. While this 'preferred reading' could in princi- ple be resisted or negotiated, the tendency was to see culture and communication as largely text-and-ideology dominated. Thus, both of the main post-structuralist bodies of cultural studies theory had, in their different ways, emphasized the power of texts over readers. Yet it was rapidly becoming clear that readers were much more active contributors to the reading process than could be counte- nanced in these models. How was this limitation to be overcome?

It was in response to such doubts that the 1980s saw a reformu- lation of the relationship between text and reader. One important contribution to this analytic shift came from feminism, which had been playing an increasingly significant role in all areas of cultural studies. In *Screen* theory, for example, the use of psychoanalytic concepts to theorize the subject had been further developed in feminist terms by Laura Mulvey in an influential and much- reprinted paper first published in 1975. I shall discuss hers and other feminist arguments in some detail in Chapter 6. Here it is only necessary to note that it was the debate precipitated by Mulvey's analysis, initially revolving around questions of gendered spectatorship, that served to open up the whole issue of active spectatorship in the subject-positioning model. Meanwhile, other forms of feminist cultural studies were focusing upon women's ability to appropriate texts and to use them in ways not necessarily consistent with the ideology that they allegedly conveyed. In exam- ining forms of 'women's culture' such as soap opera and romantic fiction, feminists exposed the tension between their textual attrib- utes as expressions of patriarchal ideology and the creative use that readers made of them in search of pleasure.

Even without these feminist interventions, however, the rise of the reader seems retrospectively inevitable in the ferment of 1980s cultural studies. Earlier ideology based models were in serious decline by mid-decade and, reacting against the perceived excesses of the past, researchers turned their attention away from the ideological power of texts and toward the individual pleasures and interpretive freedom of readers. Although the full implications of this shift are still not clear, two somewhat different ways of considering readership can be discerned. In one, so-called 'audience ethnography', the primary emphasis is methodological. By studying people's reading practices in considerable empirical detail, this approach seeks to do justice to the contextual richness of their responses. Qualitative interviewing and participant observation have become preferred methods here, with 'thick description' the analytic goal. In the other, to which the label 'cultural populism' has been applied, the main focus is upon readers' capacity to resist social pressures through inventive appropriation of culture. Critics of this view (and there are many) argue that in attending so single-mindedly to processes of cultural consumption, the theory tumbles by default into an uncritical celebration of popular culture. The radical theories from which cultural studies drew strength and originality 20 years ago are thus left high and dry. Indeed, some of those most dismayed by this turn of events have gone so far as to suggest that, in consequence, 1990s cultural studies faces a paradigm crisis. That may well be so, though, as I shall argue in Chapter 7, the causes and character of the 'crisis' are not as simple as that.

I am acutely aware of the limitations of the abbreviated story that I have just told. It omits whole sub-plots, its characters are little more than cardboard, and it has no clear ending. However, treated generously it will serve as an introductory outline for the much fuller account that is to follow. Because of the starkness of its simplification it also helps to foreground the one very general issue that has informed every stage in the development of cultural studies. I described this earlier as the tension between the structuring capacity of cultural forms and the activity of human agency, and the problem that it raises is that of establishing concepts and methods which will allow analysts to capture the interrelation of those two mutually determining features. Both main post-structuralist approaches to cultural studies tended to emphasize culture's structuring capacity. What is ideology other than the realization of that capacity in specific interests and particular cultural locations? The CCCS version, of course, was more open to considerations of active agency, but in the event lacked the concepts to make that anything more than a rhetorical possibility. The frameworks that have emerged in the wake of that failure are united in focusing upon the activity of what they variously term audiences, spectators or readers, though at the expense of structural understanding. In effect, the theoretical pendulum has swung toward agency and away from structure, thereby replacing one limiting conceptual apparatus with another. In the account that follows I shall return again and again to this question of the relationship between structure and agency. It is, I believe, the fundamental issue for any kind of cultural study.

2 *The Way We Were*

Like tribal societies, nascent disciplines are drawn to origin myths, stories which stabilize otherwise recalcitrant histories by identifying founding figures. Perhaps it is comforting to feel that one is, in Newton's memorable phrase, 'standing on the shoulders of giants', if not to see further, like Newton himself, then at least to feel the benefit of good company. The very identification of founders gives us a sense of intellectual commonality, of tradition, of aspirations shared and enemies discomfited. It offers a collective memory of the way we were, and a kind of legitimation of how we are, for although the intellectual giants of our past are not to blame for what we have done to their project, their ghosts may be (and frequently are) summoned up in support of this or that act of revision or betrayal.

So it has been with cultural studies. As the discipline has edged toward academic respectability, its history has been reconstructed and rewritten in terms of putative founders. And although Stuart Hall (1980b: 57) began one of the earliest and best known analytical accounts of the formation of cultural studies with the observation that there were no 'absolute beginnings' to be uncovered in such intellectual work, it is notable that he and most

subsequent commentators have proved more than willing to identify the likes of Richard Hoggart and Raymond Williams as key
formative influences. Consider only two of the field's better introductory texts, those by Turner (1990) and Storey (1993).
'Customarily,' Turner (1990: 12) writes, 'cultural studies is seen to
begin with the publication of Richard Hoggart's *The Uses of Literacy*
([1957] 1958) and Raymond Williams' *Culture and Society
1780–1950* ([1958] 1961) and *The Long Revolution* ([1961] 1965)',
all works which Storey (1993: 43) likewise identifies as among the
'founding texts'. These are not judgements made in haste or error,
nor are Storey and Turner unusual in making them, for most would
agree that Hoggart and Williams were indeed significant figures in
the early development of what is now called cultural studies. But
the growing inclination to conceive these writers as somehow rep-
resentative of *the* founding moment of the discipline, of its
fundamental ideas, is at best one-sided and at worst palpably misleading.

The problem does not lie with the quality or importance of their
work, of course, but with the very act of identifying founders. To
name founders is to use a convenient shorthand for the issues of
the day, but like all such conveniences it carries with it the risk of
reification: replacing a rich and varied history with reductive authorial labels. As a body of ideas cultural studies arose not from one or
two founders but from remarkably diverse sources, the more so in
that its historical roots were multi-disciplinary. To read its early history primarily in relation to Williams and Hoggart is to gloss it in
terms of only one of those disciplinary sources – important, of
course, but a single (mainly literary) thread in the early thinking of
cultural studies. The beginnings of this aspirant discipline were
much more heterogeneous than that.

Indeed, if any one analytic theme can be said to pervade all the
various early sources of cultural studies it is that of cultural

differentiation. What different forms of culture were to be found in industrial societies? What had been the impact of twentieth-century media of mass communication on those forms? How were different forms of culture related to each other? Were they stratified? Was culture in decline? Was the pervasive distinction between high and low culture meaningful and appropriate? In responding to these and related questions in the late 1950s and early 1960s, scholars from a variety of disciplinary backgrounds found themselves addressing similar issues but armed with different concepts and methods. They were the inheritors of a tradition that presupposed the value of 'high' culture and was variously concerned about its fate in twentieth-century society, but they were critical inheritors. The break with tradition that they made, the break that constituted the grounds from which cultural studies developed, crucially centred on rethinking the categories in which culture had hitherto been understood.

This process took place in a number of different intellectual contexts, two of which are the particular concern of this chapter. I shall begin with the mass society and media effects orthodoxy since that body of, on the one hand, speculative theorizing and, on the other, detailed empirical research, was crucial in much postwar criticism of twentieth-century culture. It was also the central locus for sociological thinking on this topic (other than in the then rather restricted sociologies of literature and art) and dissatisfaction with its conceptual and methodological limitations played a significant part in the early development of cultural studies. Then I shall attend to aspects of the more literary 'culture and civilization' tradition, first as it was mediated by Leavisite thinking in the 1930s and 1940s and then in relation to its influence upon Williams, Hoggart and others in their emerging concern with 'ordinary' culture. Finally, I shall try to suggest how these 'seed-bed' traditions provided fertile ground for the growth of cultural studies.

Mass society and media effects

It is difficult, undesirable even, to consider the mass society thesis and the media effects tradition in isolation from one another, since – in the USA where in the 1940s and 1950s they were given their most elaborate expression – the one tends to presuppose the basic assumptions of the other. Although mass society and mass culture arguments can be traced back illuminatingly into nineteenth-century thought (Swingewood, 1977), in the twentieth century they have been irrevocably bound up with claims about new forms of mass communication. Those arguing that modern society was becoming a mass society saw strong media effects as the *sine qua non* of 'massification', while those claiming that the media were hugely effective framed their views in the terms provided by mass society theorists. C. Wright Mills (1959: 314), himself a leading exponent of the 'manipulative' variant of the mass society thesis, catches this well.

(1) The media tell the man in the mass who he is – they give him identity; (2) they tell him what he wants to be – they give him aspirations; (3) they tell him how to get that way – they give him technique; and (4) they tell him how to feel that way even when he is not – they give him escape.

For Mills, who represents a left variation of mass society thinking, the media enabled the power elite to exert control over increasingly anonymous, passive mass-persons, with inevitable anti-democratic consequences. Of course, there were other mass society analysts who were less concerned with the directly political outcomes than was Mills, but, whatever their political persuasion, all coincided in their belief in the sheer power of media effects and in their presumption that mass society brought with it a devalued and restrictive mass culture.

It is here that we should begin, then, with the most general suppositions about culture that informed accounts of the rise of mass society and, in turn, the typical post-war approach to media effects. Culture, in this analysis, is above all a repository of value: humanity's most significant beliefs and achievements are articulated and 'stored' in culture. Or, at least, this is how it should be. But culture is not of a piece. It is differentiated, not simply in the sense that it encompasses different cultural forms, but also in the sense that such forms are perceived to be of different degrees of worth. Accordingly, culture can only properly be understood in hierarchical terms. We can and should make an evaluative distinction between, at its simplest, 'high' and 'low' culture. It is 'high' culture that carries the key values, that incorporates the richest and most significant expressions of human aspirations. 'Low' culture, by contrast, is a vulgarized product of industrial societies: commercially motivated, mass produced, and tending to pander to the lowest common denominator of taste evinced by the undiscriminating mass.

So pervasive were these assumptions that even those inclined to be positive about aspects of modern cultural life routinely adopted the hierarchical conception. Take the sociologist Edward Shils, for example, in his keynote paper given to an influential 1959 symposium. In some contrast to proponents of the orthodox mass society thesis, Shils (1961) did not see mass culture in entirely negative terms. He argued that mass society had occasioned a wider spread of what he called 'civility' and citizenship, that it had generated a growing emphasis on individual dignity, and that it had dispersed worthwhile cultural materials far more widely through society than had previously been the case. And yet even he remained unproblematically willing to distinguish between levels of culture and, perhaps more revealing, to label them in unashamedly evaluative terms. 'For present purposes,' he writes, ' we shall employ a very rough distinction among three levels of culture, which are levels of quality measured by aesthetic, intellectual, and moral standards. These are "superior" or "refined" culture, "mediocre" culture, and "brutal" culture' (Shils, 1961: 4).

Superior, mediocre, and brutal. Quite extraordinary terms for any analyst, let alone for a sociologist who might in other contexts aspire to some degree of descriptive neutrality. Yet, at the time, this usage attracted relatively little attention in as much as such bluntly evaluative distinctions were common currency in almost any discussion of culture. Hierarchical assessments were constitutive of thinking about culture, and inevitably such judgements carried with them a broadly elitist attitude to those whose taste was thus evaluated. 'Proper' culture, wherein our accumulated aesthetic and moral achievements were gathered, was seen to be at risk from the culturally impoverished mass and from those who pandered to their tastes in the media industries. Accordingly, for thinkers who accepted these terms, there was a duty to discriminate so as to protect the storehouse of human achievements and values. In some versions of the argument (well exemplified in the Leavisite work that I shall consider later) discrimination was to be cultivated with the aim of sustaining an elite capable of defending the great cultural traditions. And even those marxist theorists who saw mass culture as a tool of mass repression – as did members of the Frankfurt School who had fled to the USA from Hitler's Germany – found themselves caught in essentially elitist attitudes by virtue of the concepts that they and others routinely used to theorize culture.

So far, so familiar. But behind this well-known topography of the mass culture analysis lies a distinctive, if inconsistent, social ontology. It is distinctive in its emphasis on the determination of action by culture. As in the quotation from Mills above, social actors are largely presumed to be passive victims of the mass media, provided, as Mills puts it, with identity, aspirations, techniques and escape. As always in such top-down models they are deprived of any real sense of agency, any capacity to intervene actively in what is in effect a world pre-defined in media terms. This view is inconsistently applied, however, in that not all social actors are deprived of agency in this way. Those with the capacity to discriminate are perceived as active contributors to culture, critical, self-conscious interpreters of complex cultural artefacts. So the tacit picture here is one constructed around concepts of them and us, centre and periphery, in which the vast ordinary population of mass society are unable to resist the all-powerful constraint of the mighty media, although the fact of this constraint is immediately apparent to the enlightened and therefore resistant elite.

Here, of course, we are running up against the familiar 'hypodermic model' of media effects, that account of the functioning of the mass media which metaphorically envisages media as effective much as an injection of a powerful drug is effective: applied direct to the individual, homogeneous in character, irresistible in outcome. Now, there has been some argument as to quite how widespread were 'hypodermic' or 'magic bullet' models in mass media research in different periods, a debate I shall not seek to document in any detail here. A useful survey can be found in Bineham (1988). Suffice to say that some argue that the 'hypodermic model' was a misleading *post hoc* interpretation designed to allow later revisionists, such as Katz and Lazarsfeld (1955) and Klapper (1960, 1963), to promote their own case for limited effects against the prevailing strong effects tradition. Others, the present author included, believe that the hypodermic model was indeed an accurate reflection of much thinking in the early days of media research, and, furthermore, that the practice of effects research remained deeply influenced by these precepts throughout the various revisions of the post-war era. Certainly some such belief was shared by many critics of orthodox media research in the formative period of cultural studies, leading to a wholesale suspicion of the mass communications research tradition, a suspicion which has survived in cultural studies to this day. The question to which we must turn is, then, was this suspicion merited in relation to the underlying assumptions of mass society/media effects thinking?

Elsewhere (Tudor, 1995: 82–88) I have explored the distinctive social ontology and epistemology of effects research, and what follows is a slightly amended version of that discussion. Consider first the epistemological assumptions that underwrote the familiar methodological emphases of effects research. Effects research grew up alongside twentieth-century social sciences, at times, indeed, acting as a testing ground for their latest methodological innovations. Unsurprisingly, it exhibits many of the epistemological commitments fundamental to that disciplinary context. It shares mainstream social science's vision of scientific inquiry, one centred on the interconnected notions of theory, hypothesis and test. To know the world properly is to know it scientifically; to know it scientifically is to establish deductively interrelated propositions of empirical reference which, appropriately assessed in relation to evidence, might finally take on the status of 'laws' of human behaviour.

In practice, of course, neither effects research nor social sciences more generally lived up to this hypothetico-deductive (H-D) ideal. 'Laws' were never satisfactorily established, and hypotheses were more often *ad hoc* empirical generalizations than deduced implications of precisely formulated theories. But the fact that the H-D model was not directly reflected in most research practice did not mean that its distinctive conceptual emphases were of no significance. In three interrelated areas, in particular, it had a signal influence on the development of effects research: in its presupposition that an 'observation language' can be established to generate reliable test materials; in its assumption that propositional form was the ideal means for expressing scientific knowledge; and in its emphasis on maximizing precision of evidence. Taken together, these three legitimized an essentially empiricist research practice.

Concern to establish an adequate observation language was crucial in the development and application of the rhetoric of variables and indicators. This is not the place to rehearse the complex and chequered history of that discourse, nor to chart its analytic deficiencies; these issues have been well illuminated by Pawson (1989). Of more immediate relevance here is the tendency of variable analysis to encourage, even to legitimize, ontologies which define the social world in a manner most amenable to that approach. Thus, if behaviour is to be understood in terms of relations between variables, processes of social action are likely to be conceptualized as a concatenation of measured values scored by individuals on specified dimensions. To speak of effects, then, within such an epistemology, is to demand some form of 'before' and 'after' exposure measurement on selected scales, most commonly conducted with the naturalized individual as the primary focus.

Now add to this the supposition that the ideal form for scientific knowledge is propositional. Although the case for such a claim is firmly rooted in the deductivist view of scientific inquiry, in research practice propositional form often survived without a concomitant emphasis on deductive structure. The rigorous requirements of deductive-propositional methodologies were ameliorated by a slide toward the less demanding inductive-propositional form (Tudor, 1982: 166–168), toward what Willer and Willer (1973) call 'systematic empiricism'. Here, allegiance to the hypothetico-deductive model of scientific method is superficial. Propositions are no longer statements deduced from theory and subjected to test; they are, rather, empirical generalizations, inductively inferred using whatever are the currently accepted observation techniques. To Willer and Willer this is 'pseudo-science', an unacceptable departure from the canons of proper inquiry. If so, of course, it has to be conceded that much effects research is pseudo-scientific. But whatever the force of that claim, this divorce of processes of empirical generalization from their theoretical context gives rise to a research practice emphasizing the goal of establishing direct correlations among variables at the expense of understanding the social and psychological mechanisms which generate the correlation. In the limiting case this leads to a behaviourist focus on stimulus–response associations, and even in less restrictive conceptions it leads to a tendency to express 'findings' as superficial associative statements. Scientific knowledge thus becomes no more than an empirically buttressed assembly of such generalizations.

All this is reinforced by the familiar empiricist tendency to privilege precision, thus favouring indicators amenable to interval measurement. The most dramatic instance in effects research was the growth of content analysis during the tradition's heyday, from Berelson's (1952) concern with 'objective, systematic and quantitative' content data through developing levels of methodological sophistication and computerization (Pool, 1959; North *et al.*, 1963; Stone *et al.*, 1966; Holsti, 1969; Gerbner *et al.*, 1969). But, for all this obvious methodological invention, the processes through which media meanings were socially constructed remained largely unexplored. As it had been in other respects, effects research proved to be trapped within a somewhat restrictive empiricist epistemology, only able to envisage the communication process in terms of atomized questions about effects.

Consider, now, the social ontology presumed by this research tradition. Superficially this is less internally consistent than is its characteristic epistemology. True, it is broadly individualistic, but the form taken by that individualism varies, ranging from the stimulus–response automaton presumed in the more psychologically disposed areas of the tradition to the socialized actor common in sociologically influenced work. In the former, where the tendency has been to focus upon such features as behavioural attributes, reinforcement, and the acquisition and modification of dispositions and expectations, the 'social' is all but eliminated from the tacit ontology. The consequent difficulties of psychological effects research in generalizing from the laboratory and/or establishing consistent results are too well known to need enumeration here. Rather more interesting are the more sophisticated assumptions about *social* action which inform less psychologically restrictive approaches. Carey and Kreiling (1974), in the course of a persuasive critique of Uses and Gratifications studies, draw attention to that framework's utilitarian and functionalist underpinnings. Their diagnosis can usefully be applied more generally, for utilitarian and functionalist conceptions inform the whole effects research tradition, at least where it actively seeks to conceptualize the social.

This is to be expected. Just as effects research was epistemologically caught up in social science conceptions of scientific inquiry, so it looked to the sociological orthodoxy of the time for its social ontology. In this conception the social world is composed of actors, with ends in view, making choices among the means available to them. The terms within which they act are fundamentally structured by normative constraints and by prescriptions as to what counts as appropriate action, processes to be understood, above all, through the ubiquitous concepts of role and socialization. Role defines our social position and the normative expectations attendant upon that position, and, in the course of socialization, we internalize from our culture the norms and values proper to our roles. Systems of roles are in turn ordered into institutional structures, and these structures are interrelated in a complex system of which they constitute the building blocks. Finally, at the most general level, a broadly consensual culture ensures the continued functioning of the whole system.

Such a social ontology can be realized in a variety of ways. At its simplest it embraces vulgar normative determinism, giving rise to media research concern with the direct individual effects of mass communications on the formation and change of attitudes and values: classically, exposure studies conducted in terms of attitude scaling. Its tendency to presuppose what Wrong (1961) famously described as an 'oversocialized conception of man', to accept a view of the social actor as, in Garfinkel's (1967) phrase, a 'cultural dope', lies behind the passive manipulated audience conception of mass society theorists and their successors. More complex versions may somewhat loosen the normative bindings – as does the Uses and Gratifications approach, for example, with its emphasis on audience choices made to gratify needs – but even then the source of those needs and the criteria of choice remain fundamentally normative. Theoretically this may be an 'active audience' composed of social actors negotiating the terms of their media use, but they can only do so within the normative framework provided by the culture in question. The tacit picture remains one of socialized individuals who, as a consequence of their social circumstances, develop and seek to gratify certain needs.

Broadly, the social ontology informing effects research is one already familiar in the mainstream sociological tradition. It legitimizes a research practice which neglects questions about the social construction of meaning, seeing such issues as either technical problems of content analysis or as taken-for-granted views of the general cultural context. Variability in meaning construction and heterogeneity of culture and social practice were thus effectively excluded from consideration. Later effects research successfully sought to correct some of these limitations, but still embraced a basically top-down view of the relation between individual and society and hence between audience and communications media. Thus, even though some researchers refused to accept the mainstream's consensus model of social order, proposing instead a social world of media manipulation, social conflict and power relations, they always retained some version of the socialized actor as a central concept. Throughout effects research individuals were (and are) conceptualized as 'at the receiving end' with effects represented as general processes of socio-cultural constraint applied via the media of mass communications. This commitment at the level of tacit social ontology inevitably restricts capacity to conceptualize the complex interrelation of social agency with the larger cultural context. And even though this longer-term 'cultural effect' (Tudor, 1979) is in principle the focus for Cultivation Analysis (Gerbner and Gross, 1976; Gerbner *et al.*, 1986; Signorielli and Morgan, 1990) with its interest in the 'cultivation of culture', in practice the promise of that approach is undercut both by its empiricist epistemology and by its traditional media research ontology. The heavy television viewers central to Cultivation Analysis remain victims of culture rather than parties to the constant construction and reconstruction of their cultural environments.

How can we summarize this now rather complicated picture? One way of ordering things is to observe that the mass culture/media effects tradition has both a descriptive and an analytic version. The descriptive version is that normally encountered in public debate about mass culture and the media, both in the heyday of the mass society thesis and in the context of more recent moral panics about media effects. Here an array of often anecdotal evidence is used to buttress empirical generalizations about the power of the media to effect individual attitudes, values and behaviour. Such 'findings' are, in turn, marshalled in support of the general mass culture diagnosis. Society is openly seen as in a state of moral decline, epitomized by the contrast between the inferior products of mass culture and the authentic qualities of 'high' culture. These claims are presented as self-evident, the kind of knowledge that should be inductively apparent to any properly discriminating observer.

The analytic version, most often encountered in an academic social science context, is morally similarly disposed, but less absolute in its claims to privileged insight. Here, the assertion of powerful media effects is legitimated by the apparatus of 'science', in particular by some version of the hypothetico-deductive model. Conceptually informing such claims is the mainstream sociological commitment to a socialization model, wherein culture is the source of the key norms and values internalized by individual actors and institutionalized in the social structure. Hence, if the forms of culture are changing with the rise of mass society, then this will have far-reaching social consequences via the mechanisms of internalization and institutionalization. In principle, of course, in an approach like this that holds to an instrumental view of theory, such claims are methodologically recognized to be incomplete and partial, products of specific theoretical frameworks. But in practice, analysts all too often fall into the fallacy of misplaced concreteness, assuming that their necessarily limited knowledge-claims somehow exhaust all significant features of the reality to which they relate. Thus, although the analytic version of the mass culture/media effects tradition should in principle be more open to rational debate than the descriptive version, in the event it often falls back into a similar mode of theoretically unreflective assertiveness.

Both versions share certain key assumptions, above all a belief in the extraordinary power of mass-communicated cultural materials. In this respect they subscribe to what I earlier referred to as a 'top-down' model, one in which individual social agents are largely conceptualized as passive 'victims' of forms of transmitted culture. For this reason there is little or no recognition here that mass cultural artefacts might well be semiotically complex or that the 'audience' may play a constitutive role in meaning construction. In both descriptive and analytic versions, the concepts of the mass society/media effects tradition do not provide for the possibility that popular culture might be much richer than the typical evaluations of the tradition suggest. Nor do they allow for an agent who can be understood as an active, reflective user of culture, a knowledgeable party to the construction and reconstruction of meaning. And, in the end, it was these general limitations, along with a growing mistrust of claims to 'scientific' legitimacy for media research, that were at the root of the 1960s break with this tradition and the consequent flowering of cultural studies. But before we can pursue that event it is first necessary to consider the more 'literary' account of mass culture developed in the parallel 'culture and civilization' tradition.

Culture, discrimination and value

As with the mass society thesis, the roots of the 'culture and civilization' tradition can be traced well back into the nineteenth century. Indeed, the key twentieth-century exponent of this perspective, F. R. Leavis, begins his most famous and rhetorical of pamphlets, *Mass Civilisation and Minority Culture*, with a quotation from Matthew Arnold's 1869 volume *Culture and Anarchy*. It was Arnold ([1869] 1960: 6) who crystallized that view of culture as 'the best that has been thought and said in the world', and who laid the foundations for an analysis that saw industrialization and the concomitant rise of the 'mass' as a profound threat to culture and civilization. It was also Arnold who saw a key role for education – 'the road to culture', as he described it (1960: 209) – in combating cultural decline and in ensuring the preservation of a stable status quo. However, it is the spirit rather than the detail of Arnold's views that inform this century's embodiment of the 'culture and civilization' position, so I shall here concentrate on the mediation of these ideas in the work of Leavis and his associates. They address concerns about distinctively twentieth-century culture and they were hugely influential, if indirectly, in forming the 'literary' context in which cultural studies first developed.

Leavis himself wrote abundantly on a range of literary and cultural topics, much of his work appearing initially in the journal *Scrutiny* in the 1930s. *Scrutiny* represented a crucial moment in literary and cultural criticism in the English-speaking world (Mulhern, 1979) and served as a focus for the emergence of what might loosely be called 'Leavisism'. For my present purposes, Leavisism can be understood as having two main components: a general cultural critique and, not unrelated, a body of detailed analysis and evaluation of literary and cultural texts. I shall begin this account by briefly examining the familiar features of Leavisism's cultural critique, and then go on to consider some aspects of the critical methodology that Leavis developed in the course of his specific analyses. Both features had an important impact on early cultural studies.

The basic terms of Leavis' position are made very clear on the first page of *Mass Civilisation and Minority Culture*. 'In any period,' he writes, 'it is upon a very small minority that the discerning appreciation of art and literature depends' (Leavis, 1930: 3). But this minority's significance extends beyond their capacity to appreciate 'art and literature' for they constitute 'the consciousness of the race' (*ibid*: 4). He continues in similar vein:

> Upon this minority depends our power of profiting by the finest human experience of the past; they keep alive the subtlest and most perishable parts of the tradition. Upon them depend the implicit

standards that order the finer living of an age, the sense that this is worth more than that, this rather than that is the direction in which to go, that the centre is here rather than there. (*ibid*: 5)

They are the guardians of culture and, in the twentieth century, this culture is in crisis. It is in crisis because of larger social changes which, first in America but increasingly in other countries, have spread mass production and standardization across wide reaches of modern society, undermining what elsewhere Leavis and Thompson (1933) write of as the 'organic community'. In newspapers, in broadcasting, in advertizing, in film, we encounter 'that deliberate exploitation of the cheap response which characterises our civilisation' (Leavis, 1930: 11). Though there may be room for hope that we can climb out of what the contemporary critic I. A. Richards identified as a 'cultural trough', it is clear that for Leavis the challenge is considerable: '[t]he prospects of culture, then, are very dark' (*ibid*: 30).

What is to be done? Q. D. Leavis (1932: 211) suggests the thrust of a response. 'It is only by acquiring access to good poetry, great drama, and the best novels, the forms of art that, since they achieve their effects through language, most readily improve the quality of living, that the atmosphere in which we live may be oxygenated.' If such access can be enabled, if the reading public, with whom she is particularly concerned in this study, can be weaned away from popular fiction and into a proper appreciation of the 'best literature', perhaps the cultural crisis can be overcome. Not surprisingly, then, Leavisism is much exercised by education and by the attempt to train critical awareness. Both in seeking to influence educational practice by providing (in Leavis and Thompson's *Culture and Environment*) a handbook for the use of teachers wanting to promote a critical response to contemporary media materials, and in the detailed textual analysis that came to characterize the Leavisite critical 'method', they sought to sustain civilization by encouraging discrimination. In so doing they deeply influenced the character of literary education in Britain.

The similarity of this analysis to that found in the mass society/media effects tradition is quite obvious. Both views see modern society in crisis; both see that crisis as emerging from specific features of industrial societies; both see culture and taste as stratified; and both are deeply unsympathetic to the products of new, twentieth-century forms of popular culture. The Leavisite view is distinctive, however, in three main respects. First, it supposes that an ideal form of social organization is possible, an organic community within which people may live as 'integral parts'. The positive value placed on this way of life is apparent in the use that Leavis and Thompson (1933) make of the work of Sturt who, as 'George Bourne', had written somewhat romantically of the rich traditions of rural civilization. However, lest the wrong impression be given, it should be noted that Leavisism is more inclined to bemoan the loss of organic living (and praise its expression in D. H. Lawrence) than to propose utopian alternatives to modernity. Theirs is not a revolutionary doctrine in pursuit of primitive communalism.

Secondly, they are distinctive in the emphasis they place upon education and the promotion of critical awareness. In spite of the tone of apocalyptic dismay that pervades the 1930s work, Leavisism retains a degree of optimism about the possibility of defending and developing culture. Although clearly elitist in their views about the role of the educated minority, they were not backward in condemning the pretensions and lack of discrimination among those who conventionally laid claim to 'high' culture. The capacity for discrimination was not inherited, or a necessary function of class – it was learned. So, if critical awareness could and should be taught, as they argue, then that suggests an implicit humanist commitment to, if not the perfectibility, then at least the positive potential of human activity. In this respect Leavisism retains a rather stronger conception of human agency than is found in other mass culture formulations. For example, in distinguishing his views from marxist theories of culture, Leavis (1952: 184) claims that although 'material conditions count, there is a certain measure of spiritual autonomy in human affairs, and [that] human intelligence, choice and will do really and effectively operate, expressing an inherent human nature'. To be concerned with literature, he continues, is to recognize the importance of the creative individual and 'the truth that it is only in individuals that society lives' (*ibid*: 185).

Thirdly, Leavisism is distinct in its development of a method of close textual analysis which, although centrally concerned to expose the virtues or failings of literary works, is also generally applicable to other forms of culture. Though their aim is hardly one of approbation, the examples of modern cultural materials that Leavis and Thompson (1933) put forward for teachers' use are designed to be examined using Leavisism's distinctive critical apparatus. It is the use of this method that later leads to so-called 'left-Leavisism' – the application of close textual analysis to popular cultural forms with a view to revealing their positive qualities rather than demonstrating their destructive impact on civilized values. Given the significance of that development for the emergence of cultural studies, it is necessary here to examine the distinctive features of the 'Leavisite method' a little more closely. So what is (or was) Leavisite method?

The question is difficult to answer in short compass. One can point to, say, the analyses of George Eliot, Henry James and Joseph Conrad that form the bulk of *The Great Tradition* (Leavis, 1960) as instances of his 'method' in action, but this begs the question: what is it that distinguishes this approach? Revealingly, Leavis himself was always reluctant to formulate his position in general terms. In his response to Wellek's (1937) philosophical demand that he lay bare his assumptions and produce a theory in their defence, he falls back on the notion that what is required of philosophy is very different to that which is required of literary criticism. One must avoid the pernicious consequences of 'queering one discipline with the habits of another' (Leavis, 1952: 213) and so resist the temptation to formulate general axioms of method. Leavis does grant that, over time, the critic may achieve consistency and coherence from which abstract principles may be inferred, but this is not the purpose of the critical enterprise. Leavis has quite other goals.

> I hoped, by putting in front of them [readers of poetry], in a criticism that should keep as close to the concrete as possible, my own developed 'coherence of response', to get them to agree (with, no doubt, critical qualifications) that the map, the essential order, of English poetry seen as a whole did, when they interrogated their experience, look like that to them also. Ideally I ought perhaps . . . to be able to complete the work with a theoretical statement. But I am sure that the kind of work that I have attempted comes first, and would, for such a theoretical statement to be worth anything, have to be done first. (*ibid*: 214)

I have quoted this passage because it encompasses so many features of Leavis' tacit epistemology. One should keep close to the concrete, to – a favoured concept this – experience. Theoretical statements can only be arrived at (if they should be advanced at all) after the fact: only when the critic has done the work of concrete textual analysis might there be a place for theory. The idea that theoretical presuppositions inform, even constitute, the grounds on which concrete analysis is built is bypassed in the claim that the work comes first. Leavis' methodology, then, is a form of inductivism. The skilled observer (critic) examines and explores the concrete material (poetry) and lays bare its 'essential order'. And then the readers are invited to 'interrogate their experience' so that they might agree that yes, indeed, the critic has revealed that all-important coherence.

This last stage is the interrogative method, the famous 'this is so, is it not?' The critic works with concrete judgements, detailed analyses of the text, and appeals to the readers' shared experience to 'get them to agree': 'This – doesn't it? – bears such a relation to that; this kind of thing – don't you find it so? – wears better than that' (Leavis, 1952: 215). But, as Anderson (1968: 52) points out, '[t]he central idea of this epistemology – the interrogative statement – demands one crucial precondition: a shared, stable system of beliefs and values'. Where critic and readers do not hold to the same beliefs, presuppositions, theoretical commitments, then – as with all forms of inductive empiricism – meaningful discourse is no longer possible except (perhaps) at the level of meta-analysis. Hence the need for explicit theoretical and methodological discussion. If there is a community of culture shared by critic and reader the detailed textual argument can be experienced as persuasive. But if there is no such community, then the critic's claims will seem to the unsympathetic reader to be no more than arbitrary assertions of one viewpoint over another. In this way Leavis' faith in the significance of the 'organic community' finds an odd reflection in his epistemology, and his method, in turn, forms the basis for Leavisism's educational mission. If we could only be educated into embracing Leavis' values and critical perceptions, the argument runs, then we would indeed come to constitute a cultured community.

In the end, then, and for the moment leaving to one side his positive commitment to the significance of human agency, the underlying ideas of Leavisism have similar limitations to those of the mass society/media effects tradition. Both traditions are firmly empiricist, in Leavis' case in an openly inductive and anti-theoretical form, and in the case of effects research somewhat disguised by a formal adherence to the hypothetico-deductive view of theory which, in practice, turns out to have no real methodological consequences. Also, both are unable to grapple constructively with the remarkable cultural differentiation characteristic of modern societies, leading them to the familiar error of misperceiving all cultural change as cultural decline. And even though there is no intrinsic reason why Leavisite method, in the form of close textual analysis, should not constructively be applied to popular culture, Leavis' own somewhat apocalyptic views on the failings of mass culture run counter to any such application. Some of those he influenced, however, were less restricted in this respect, and in the 1950s the terms of the culture and civilization tradition began to shift.

Initially, at least, the representatives of the changing tradition retained the familiar Leavisite desire to encourage discrimination among forms of culture and, through education, to ensure that new generations were appropriately equipped to adopt an attitude of critical evaluation. They also retained a positive humanistic view of the social agent as a creative force, though this was now applied to a wider social range than had been apparent in Leavisism's ingrained elitism. And they retained much of Leavisite epistemology, both in their continuing emphasis on the necessity for close textual analysis and in their tendency to hold to a somewhat unreflective and pragmatic empiricism on the question of the role and function of theorising. Where they began to differ most seriously was not on these general epistemological and ontological commitments, but on the basic evaluation of culture. Though still sharing the founding Leavisite moral concern about the need for a critical response to undesirable features of twentieth-century culture, Hoggart (1958), Williams (1961) and Hall and Whannel (1964) rejected the tradition's out-and-out elitism, arguing that there were forms of popular culture which were of sufficient significance to merit close attention. Quite what was thus identified proved variable. Hoggart, for example, was particularly positive about the working-class cultures within which he had spent his youth, but much less tolerant of those adopted by his post-war successors. His chapter headings capture that bilious tone, contrasting, for instance, 'The "Real" World of People' and 'The Full Rich Life' with his characterization of 'newer mass art' in terms like 'Invitations to a Candy-Floss World' and 'Sex in Shiny Packets'.

Yet in the context of the 'culture and civilization' tradition *The Uses of Literacy* does indeed make some progress toward a less restrictive conception of culture. However, it is in Raymond Williams' contributions to rethinking the tradition that the real potential for change can best be seen. Williams was a complex and striking thinker, the more so if one seeks to follow him right through the long voyage of his engagement with the idea of culture. I shall be unjust to him here, considering only those elements in his work of the late 1950s and early 1960s that crystallized some of the terms through which the 'culture and civilization' tradition could be transcended. For Williams it was a matter of fundamental conviction that, in the title of a famous 1958 essay, 'Culture is ordinary' (Williams, 1989). In the light of this commitment, and perhaps somewhat disingenuously, he professed himself puzzled by the desire of so many to mark off culture as separate from the experiences of ordinary people in their daily lives. The 'mass', condemned by both the mass society and the 'culture and civilization' traditions to a life bereft of culture, were, to Williams, real people actually living their cultures. 'There are in fact no masses;' he writes, 'there are only ways of seeing people as masses' (Williams, 1961: 289). This did not mean that he had a uniformly positive view of modern culture. Like Hoggart, he certainly did not, always maintaining the importance of adopting a critical attitude to undesirable features of any culture. But he saw that the differentiation of culture was much more complex and significant than prevailing traditions of thought had hitherto grasped, and in *Culture and Society 1780–1950* and *The Long Revolution* he set out to examine and rethink those traditions.

This led him into a lengthy consideration of the concept of culture, first in terms of its historical development (especially within the 'culture and civilization' tradition) and then, more abstractly, with a view to developing appropriate concepts and methods for its understanding. It is the latter that particularly concerns me here, and its major locus is to be found in the first part of *The Long Revolution*. Hall (1980a: 19) rightly describes this book as a 'text of the break' and as 'a seminal event in English post-war intellectual life'. It is here that Williams (1965: 57–58) spells out most clearly his well-known three definitions of culture: the 'ideal', where culture is concerned with perfection in terms of absolute values; the 'documentary', where culture is a body of work capturing human thought and experience; and the 'social', where culture refers to a distinctive way of life. To examine culture is, for Williams, to examine all these aspects.

> Cultural history must be more than the sum of the particular histories, for it is with the relations between them, the particular forms of the whole organization, that it is especially concerned. I would then define the theory of culture as the study of relationships between elements in a whole way of life. The analysis of culture is the attempt to discover the nature of the organization which is the complex of these relationships. (*ibid*: 63)

'Pattern', he suggests, is an essential focus for this cultural analysis, both characteristic patterns of culture themselves and the relationships that link such patterns. Invoking Fromm's concept of 'social character' and Benedict's 'patterns of culture', he searches for terms to describe what for him is the central distinguishing feature of the phenomenon: 'a particular sense of life, a particular community of experience hardly needing expression, through which the characteristics of our way of life that an external analyst could describe are in some way passed, giving them a particular and characteristic colour' (*ibid*: 64). The distinctiveness of this 'community of experience' is not captured by 'social character' or 'pattern of culture' which terms, for Williams, lack the appropriate experiential dimension. The alternative expression that he proposes is 'structure of feeling'.

It is not always easy to grasp quite how 'structure of feeling' differs from, say, pattern of culture. In part it is to do with abstraction. Social character and pattern of culture are, for Williams, the terms of an external analyst abstracting pattern from concrete social activities. Structure of feeling, on the other hand, seeks to capture something about the 'actual experience' in which these abstract patterns are lived. Yet when Williams claims to detect a 'popular structure of feeling' in, for example, the novels of the 1840s (*ibid*: 81–86) he, too, is inevitably abstracting from the 'lived culture'. There is surely an epistemological confusion here, stemming perhaps from Williams' failure (at this stage of his work) to consider more openly the status and role of theorizing. Hall (1980a: 19) observes of *The Long Revolution* that 'it attempted to graft on to an idiom and mode of discourse irredeemably particular, empirical and moral in emphasis, its own highly individual kind of "theorizing"'. This is an apposite description, catching both the strength of the empiricism and moral concern inherited from Leavisism and Williams' feeling that, although theoretical reflection was so much more than an unnecessary afterthought to the real work of analysis, it still had to be, as it were, contained within that work if misleading abstraction was to be avoided. In invoking 'structure of feeling' he seeks to work from within the cultural terms in which real lives are lived, yet seems reluctant to concede that this account is no less abstract, no less irreducibly theoretical, than that offered by Fromm or Benedict or, indeed, any other analyst. In summarizing his aims he writes (Williams, 1965: 319): '[w]e have been trying to develop methods of analysis which, over a range from literature to social institutions, can articulate actual structures of feeling – the meanings and values which are lived in works and relationships – and clarify the processes through which these structures form and change.' Yet even a generously disposed reader of *The Long Revolution* would be hard pressed to say exactly what constitutes these distinctive 'methods of analysis', a task not helped by Williams' almost Leavisite insistence in the Foreword to the 1965 Penguin edition that 'the method is in this sense the substance'.

Later, of course, Williams was to reflect much more fully upon theoretical issues in the context of his continuing concern with developments in modern marxism. But at this stage, and for all the extraordinary invention and insight of *The Long Revolution*, questions of theory and method have not yet quite escaped the inheritance of the culture and civilization tradition. On substantive issues, however, Williams makes remarkable progress. He moves the terms of discussion of culture toward a much less restrictive conception than was prevalent in either of the main traditions that I have been discussing in this chapter, convincingly demonstrating the necessity of understanding the totality of relations between society, art and activity. He establishes the centrality of communication processes to community and common culture, a topic taken up, if somewhat unevenly, in his next book on communications (Williams, 1962). And he extends even further the emphasis on human agency that threads its way through the culture and civilization tradition. 'We must not think only of society or the group acting on the unique individual,' he writes, 'but also of many unique individuals, through a process of communication, creating and where necessary extending the organization by which they will continue to be shaped' (Williams, 1965: 117). It is this tension between and interdependence of individual agency and the structures that people inherit and recreate that will continue to haunt the emerging discipline of cultural studies.

Appropriating art

By the mid-1960s many of the views shared by the mass society and culture and civilization traditions were increasingly subject to scepticism among a younger generation of scholars working in a variety of disciplinary contexts. They rejected the cultural elitism of both traditions, in part because of a growing tendency to reject traditional forms of elitism *per se*, and in part because of the recognition that, methodologically, elitist cultural commitments had blinded analysts to the richness of so many popular cultural forms. This had resulted in, on the one hand, media research relying upon mechanistic methods of content analysis that proved entirely unable to capture the complexity of communication processes, and, on the other hand, 'literary critical' discussions that simply condemned popular culture, sight unseen. Like Williams – though not always directly influenced by him – the new generation felt that it was essential to understand culture as deeply embedded in people's social lives, as part and parcel of everyday experience rather than something to be aesthetically differentiated in order to supply the pleasures of a cultured elite. But, as yet, there was neither a theoretical nor a methodological focus for this growing sense of dissatisfaction with received views on culture, and for a period the main thrust of dissent took the unlikely but understandable form of legitimating the study of popular culture by demonstrating its significance within traditional evaluative terms. So-called left-Leavisism is a good instance of this in action, at least if that somewhat ambiguous label encompasses the strategy adopted by, for example, Hall and Whannel (1964).

This approach could generally be described as one of appropriation. If only one can demonstrate, it assumes, that specific popular forms are works of quality when measured against established critical standards, then hitherto ignored works of popular culture can be appropriated under the rubric of art. So, Hall and Whannel (1964: 67) are eager not to base evaluations 'on the institutions [of mass media] but on the quality of the work done within them'. In this way, they suggest, genuine popular art can be distinguished from the formulaic products of mass art. Much of their book is devoted to detailed analyses of individual cases, where the educational intent and even the language of critical discussion itself recalls the central concerns of the Leavisite tradition. Lacking both a coherent theorization of culture and an adequate methodology for analysing the textual materials with which it is concerned, *The Popular Arts* may now seem confused in its attempt to distinguish between the various forms of popular art and somewhat sententious in its critical evaluations. In 1964, however, its insistence on taking popular forms seriously represented a significant step away from the restrictions of the orthodox tradition.

This strategy of appropriation was given perhaps its most thoroughgoing expression in application to film. There was, after all, a well-established critical tradition that had for many years sought to demonstrate that the cinema should be recognized as 'the seventh art'. Historically that had largely been based on a case for the film director as 'author' and for 'art cinema' as superior to the typical conveyor-belt products of Hollywood, a view firmly established by the 1950s. In the 1960s, however, there was a distinctive shift in the evaluation of what might properly count as 'art' in film: a new generation of film critics foregrounded the work of hitherto undervalued Hollywood directors, and sought to demonstrate the point by subjecting their films to detailed critical evaluation. In some cases that work, too, was overtly influenced by the Leavisite tradition. So, for example, in detailed textual studies of the films of Howard Hawks and Alfred Hitchcock the then Leavis-influenced critic Robin Wood (1968, 1969) sought to demonstrate the profundity, the organicism, the universal significance of their work. Not averse to making strong claims – *'Vertigo* seems to me to be Hitchcock's masterpiece to date, and one of the four or five most profound and beautiful films the cinema has yet given us' (Wood, 1969: 71) – Wood set for film criticism the same high standards of detailed analysis that the Leavisite tradition had applied to literature. But, once more, as a contemporary discussion of Wood's work put it, '[t]he result is a critical method which avoids developing an analytic and evaluative apparatus' (Lovell, 1969: 44).

Again and again in the 1960s this theme emerges, both in the lively debate that distinguished the world of film studies, and in more general considerations of culture. As a new generation reacted against the received wisdom of the past, they increasingly recognized that it was not just the elitism of mass culture views that was at fault. It was also – perhaps even above all – their empiricism that confounded any attempt to stand back from the process of analysis itself and debate the terms in which understanding of culture was to be constructed. The call was for theory. Theory which would locate cultural phenomena in the larger context of which they were a part. Theory which would provide a fresh and less restrictive understanding of communication. Theory which would underwrite a method of analysis capable of the fine discriminations necessary if interpretation and meaning construction were to be understood. In a word, a theory which would draw together into one body of thought the growing interest in the various *languages* of modern culture. But, in the enthusiasm to meet these challenges few noticed that the term 'theory' was rapidly developing a whole range of meanings, not all of them consistent with each other or even within themselves. And what this meant, of course, was that when, in the guise of structuralism, a potential theory of language and communication did emerge, it rapidly came to mean very different things to different people. From this epistemological diversity emerged many of the distinctive strengths and failings of cultural studies. But that is another story and another chapter.

3 *Enter Structuralism*

As befits a topic as vast and as often misrepresented as structuralism, let me begin with a sweeping generalization. The most striking developments in twentieth-century thought, at least in the humanities and the social sciences, derive much of their force and originality from the so-called 'linguistic turn'. This is not to say that there are no significant developments in psychology, in literary studies, in philosophy, in history, in sociology, which do not emerge from this century's fascination with language. Of course there are. But if one were to seek a single intellectual common cause, a shared thread of thought which has influenced so many of the disciplines concerned with human activity and its products, then language would surely be that topic.

Most of these disciplines have not, however, conceived language in uniform terms. Indeed, at different times the published works of scholars as diverse as Whorff, Wittgenstein, Chomsky, Bernstein, Saussure, Austin, Garfinkel and Hjelmslev (to select a wilfully mixed bunch) have contradicted each other while also influencing academic worlds far beyond those envisaged by their original authors. So, although language has indeed emerged as a shared cross-disciplinary focus, the concepts invoked for its understanding have varied hugely, and while the expression 'linguistic turn' may articulate a common interest, it has not brought with it any final agreement on the theories and methods essential to the proper study of language. What it did bring, however, was an extraordinary invention and intellectual excitement to the challenge of understanding the workings of language.

It was in this context that in the later 1960s the youthful discipline of cultural studies was casting about for an innovative approach to culture, and in such circumstances it is hardly surprising that the topic of language came to the fore. The 'linguistic turn' was well established, cultural phenomena clearly used language and were themselves language-like, and the emergent focus of cultural studies on the ways in which meaning was constructed in different cultural forms had an obvious affinity with at least some approaches to analysing language. But which approach would best serve the ambitions of the nascent discipline? With a bewildering variety from which to choose, it was initially by no means obvious where effort should be directed. However, as the decade progressed it became increasingly apparent to English-speaking scholars that a dominantly French movement – structuralism – had a provocative contribution to make to thinking about language, communication and culture. The anthropologist Claude Lévi-Strauss – of whom more later – had played a vital role in carrying word of structuralism to an audience beyond linguistics, and other French scholars were also attracting attention outside their own country. In the pages of the French journal *Communications*, for instance, Barthes, Bremond and Greimas were applying structuralist methods to narrative forms, and in film studies especially (notably through the work of Christian Metz) there was a growing interest in the methods of semiology – the science of signs.

In the beginning, though, there was much confusion about

precisely what made structuralism distinctive, and in most disciplines the guardians of older traditions were determinedly resistant to these exotic Gallic imports. Sociologists, for example, claimed with some irritation that they had always been 'structuralist', but in so doing failed to recognize that the concept of structure as it had developed in sociology was quite different to the relational concept that exercised Lévi-Strauss and the other French structuralists. In English literary studies, an area already well known for ferocious academic invective, there was even a period when to be a structuralist was tantamount to treachery, and those so labelled found themselves marginalized by the critical orthodoxy. It was only when the English-speaking world began to examine the roots of structuralist ideas in the work of the Swiss linguist Ferdinand de Saussure that the smoke of battle began to clear and the full potential of structuralism became apparent. Saussure's work had long been familiar in linguistics, but its more general implications for the study of culture only emerged in Anglo-American scholarship at the end of the 1960s and in the early 1970s, and even then largely in mediated form. It is to Saussure, therefore, that we must first turn in seeking to understand the chequered history of structuralism's impact on cultural studies.

The Saussurian foundation

I shall not pretend to give a balanced and comprehensive account of Saussure's ideas. Such exegesis is available elsewhere – as a starting point Culler (1986) is as good as any – and, in any case, it is Saussure's theories as they were modified and understood by cultural studies that are mainly of interest here. Nevertheless, even with this limited aim, it is worth observing that Saussure is not entirely well served by the circumstances of publication of his most influential work (*Cours de linguistique générale*) and by the various attempts to translate his key terms into English. The *Cours* was first published in 1916, three years after Saussure's death, and was based not on any manuscript that he left but on lecture notes taken by his students. In consequence, there has been plenty of room for Saussure scholars to argue that the editors of the *Cours* misrepresented Saussure at key points, or presented his theories in an order which would not have been embraced by the theorist himself. Such argument has been fed by subsequent publication of some of the lecture notes on which the original editors based their synthesis (Saussure, 1993, 1996), providing new opportunities for readers to make their own critical reconstructions. However, since it is the *Cours* as originally formulated which so influenced the rise of structuralism, it will be on that version that I shall base my discussion.

The problem of translation is less easily resolved. Translators and borrowers of Saussure's concepts have often struggled to find acceptable English equivalents, most notably in relation to his pivotal use of the term *langue* and his account of the components of the sign. In Roy Harris' translation (Saussure, 1983), which I shall use here, *langue* is variably translated according to context, sometimes as 'the language' but more often as something like 'linguistic structure' or 'language as a structured system'. One can readily sympathize with Harris since the term itself is used variably in the *Cours* and there is no direct equivalent in English. I shall resort to the now common escape route of using *langue* untranslated, if necessary quoting the original French from the Payot edition (Saussure, 1969). Notable differences are also found in translations of Saussure's terms *signifié* and *signifiant*. Harris uses 'signification' and 'signal' to translate these two, but since much of the cultural studies literature has gravitated toward the more clumsy 'signified' and 'signifier' I shall follow that practice. There are also other issues of translation and usage. *Les rapports associatifs*, for example, appropriately translated as 'associative relations', has mutated over the years into 'paradigmatic relations' as part of a contrast pairing with 'syntagmatic'. However, such matters of detail need not concern us here. I shall draw attention to them if it becomes relevant, but compared to the task of adequately rendering *langue* they are almost trivial.

Let us turn to the substance of Saussure's project. Like Durkheim, his equally remarkable French contemporary in sociology, Saussure was committed to science and to scientific method. It is notable, therefore, that when he criticizes his comparative linguistics predecessors it is because, in spite of their considerable achievements, 'they did not manage to found a *true science* of linguistics' (Saussure, 1983: 3, my emphasis). More specifically, they failed to define precisely their topic of study. Many of the concepts that Saussure introduces, and the key distinctions that he goes on to make, relate first of all to distinguishing the proper subject matter of scientific linguistics and, in due course, of the discipline that he dubs 'semiology'. Nor is science for Saussure simply a matter of systematic description, a characteristically nineteenth-century form of inductive empiricism concerned to chart the history and variety of languages in use. He has larger and more abstract aims than that: 'to determine the forces operating permanently and universally in all languages [*toutes les langues*], and to formulate general laws which account for all particular linguistic phenomena historically attested' (*ibid*: 6). To do so, he considers it necessary to identify linguistics' proper object of study and it is here that the first of Saussure's famous distinctions comes into play – that between *langue* and *parole*.

The essence of this distinction lies in two aspects of the operation of language. Clearly, we speak. That is to say, as individuals we articulate certain sequences of sounds over which, more or less, we have control. This speech has a material existence in time and, in appropriate circumstances, it may be comprehended by those who encounter it. Speech itself, of course, is individual – 'an individual act of the will and the intelligence' (*ibid*: 14) – but the capacity to speak in such a way as to be understood and, in turn, to understand others' speech, is a social phenomenon, a consequence of the shared, structuring character of language. So, the heart of the matter lies in distinguishing, on the one hand, specific articulations (*parole* or, in a generalized sense of the term, speech) which are made using the terms of a language, from, on the other hand, the language system (*langue*), the structuring apparatus which enables us to speak meaningfully in the first place. 'By distinguishing between the language itself and speech [*En séparant la langue de la parole*], we distinguish at the same time: (1) what is social from what is individual, and (2) what is essential from what is ancillary and more or less accidental' (*ibid*: 13–14).

For Saussure it is *langue*, linguistic structure, which is the proper subject matter of linguistics. It exists independently of any specific individual articulation for, as he repeatedly insists, *langue* refers to the social and collective aspect of language. In effect, it is the system of codes and conventions which makes intelligible speech possible. If I speak and you understand, then that is because we share access to a *langue*, and it is precisely that shared access which enables us to communicate. *Langue*, then, is crucially distinctive. 'It is not, in our opinion, simply the same thing as language. Linguistic structure is only one part of language, even though it is an essential part. The structure of a language is a social product of our language faculty. At the same time, it is also a body of necessary conventions adopted by society to enable members of society to use their language faculty' (*ibid*: 9–10). It is, Saussure adds, both a system in itself and a principle of classification.

Saussure's insistence that the proper subject matter of

linguistics is *langue* has radical consequences for the study of language. It underlines the irreducibly social character of language, an achievement in itself, but it also gives much greater force to the argument for the necessity of theory and, thereby, to a more deductively inclined epistemology than was common in nineteenth-century thought. Since *langue* is the 'absent' system which makes speech possible, it cannot be apprehended directly but only through its instantiations in speech. In effect, then, the study of *langue* requires us to develop theoretical models of its systems of codes and conventions and to demonstrate that such models adequately capture the capacity of language systems to enable speech. And although Saussure himself (in the passage quoted earlier) writes of discovering 'forces operating universally' and 'general laws' when he characterizes the goals of linguistics, the thrust of his detailed analysis suggests a rather more holistic relation between model and evidence than might be expected from such a mechanistically influenced view of science. It is the system as a whole which enables speech, and its systemic quality cannot, without loss, be reduced to the propositional form characteristic of sciences primarily concerned to establish law statements. I am not suggesting here that Saussure consciously anticipated changes in scientific epistemology which would only become clear later in the century – only that part of the innovative quality of his work is that in its conceptual apparatus it presupposes a view of theory and method which, at that time, was still relatively undeveloped.

He is also fully aware that the argument he advances for the study of *langue* is more generally applicable to other systems of signs. 'A language is a system of signs expressing ideas, and hence comparable to writing, the deaf-and-dumb alphabet, symbolic rites, forms of politeness, military signals, and so on. It is simply the most important of such systems' (*ibid*: 15). He envisages the possibility of a science which will examine all these sign-systems, studying their role in social life. This as yet non-existent science he calls semiology, and he conceives it as part of social psychology. Natural language is a special type of system within this semiological domain, and his interest in it – and, presumably, the conceptual apparatus that he develops for analysing language – is essentially semiological. That is, he is first of all concerned to understand those features that are common to all systems of signification. Any system of signs functions as a communicative process in consequence of its own structuring system – its *langue*-like set of codes and conventions – and the task of semiology is to explore the operation of such systems in their social context.

This immediately raises the question of what is to constitute the basic unit of a semiological system – namely, what is a sign? Saussure's answer involves a further famous distinction, that between *signifié* and *signifiant* or, in the now conventional English rendering, signified and signifier respectively. The linguistic sign, Saussure argues, is double-sided, always containing two elements. It does not connect a name to an object, as some correspondence views have tended to suggest, but links the concept carried by the sign with the sound-pattern through which the sign is given expression. To avoid ambiguity, Saussure replaces 'sound-pattern' and 'concept' with the more abstract terms 'signifier' and 'signified', a choice which also has the effect of highlighting the applicability of this distinction to all significatory systems and not just to the linguistic sign. Whatever the concrete material of which they are composed, all signs involve both a signified and a signifier.

This leads on to a key claim given succinct expression in Saussure's blunt declaration that 'the linguistic sign is arbitrary' (*ibid*: 67). When first encountered this assertion can seem rather puzzling, partly because of the overtones of randomness in the word 'arbitrary', something of which Saussure was himself aware. To clarify his claim, he expands on the idea of arbitrariness in terms of seeing the signifier as unmotivated, as having no 'natural' connection to the signified. The idea 'cat' has no intrinsic link with the sequence of sounds c-a-t; the connection is conventional and has been socially established. Of course, there are systems using signs that are to some degree non-arbitrary or 'natural'. Saussure mentions mime as an example, and later in the *Cours* finds it necessary to distinguish between absolute and relative arbitrariness, conceding even that 'the sign may be motivated to a certain extent' (*ibid*: 130). Interestingly, this problem was to re-emerge in later applications of semiology in cultural studies, where, for instance, considerable energies were devoted to considering whether and in what degree the relation of photographic (and cinematic) signifiers to their signifieds could be described as arbitrary. But the more immediate significance of Saussure's concept of the arbitrary sign is twofold: it again underscores the socially relative character of signification systems, and it leads us toward a concept of language as a relational system of differences.

On the former, this passage sums up the generality and social significance of the claim of arbitrariness:

the main object of study in semiology will [none the less] be the class of systems based upon the arbitrary nature of the sign. For any means of expression accepted in a society rests in principle upon a collective habit, or on convention, which comes to the same thing. Signs of politeness, for instance, although often endowed with a certain natural expressiveness (prostrating oneself nine times on the ground is the way to greet an emperor in China) are none the less fixed by rule. It is this rule which renders them obligatory, not their intrinsic value. We may therefore say that signs which are entirely arbitrary convey better than others the ideal semiological process. (*ibid*: 68)

This 'ideal semiological process' rests on a *langue*, of course, and is composed of elements carrying meaning by virtue of their (conventional) relations with each other. As Saussure understands it, the sign is not simply an isolated and arbitrary combination of sound and concept. It takes on what he calls 'linguistic value' in consequence of its position in the system of which it is a part just as, in a comparison of which he is fond, the pieces in chess take on their value in consequence not of some individual character that they bring *to* the system but because of their position *within* the system. A knight, he points out, could be replaced by any material object, since its value in the game, its identity, is not a consequence of its physical character but of its position in relation to other chess pieces and to the conventions which constitute the game (*ibid*: 108–109). So it is with language. The linguistic value of a word, for instance, depends in a given language on the words which express 'neighbouring ideas'. He takes as an instance the French word *mouton* and the English word *sheep* which, although taken as mutually translatable, have different linguistic values (*ibid*: 114). In English there is the separate word *mutton* for the cooked meat of the animal, whereas in French *mouton* encompasses both the beast and the meat. The difference in value of *mouton* and *sheep*, then, flows from the difference of positioning of the words in their respective systems – they are defined by comparison with other contiguous terms. As he puts it, perhaps somewhat rhetorically: '[i]n the language itself, there are only differences' (*ibid*: 118). And it is the whole system of differences that defines its component elements; not the component elements that define the system. Significatory units are defined relationally.

This central concern with relations – '[i]n a linguistic state, then, everything depends on relations' (*ibid*: 121) – leads Saussure to yet another of his influential distinctions. He differentiates between what he terms syntagmatic and associative aspects of the relations between linguistic units. A syntagma (*syntagme*) is a sequenced combination in which the units follow each other in a linear fashion: words in a sentence, say, or sounds constituting a signifier. Associative relations, on the other hand, exist not between units linked in linear sequences in the here-and-now but between units which are connected by 'mental association' and which are, thereby, made available for use in particular syntagmas. Saussure uses a building metaphor to enlarge upon his distinction. 'A column is related in a certain way to the architrave it supports. This disposition, involving two units co-present in space, is comparable to a syntagmatic relation. On the other hand, if the column is Doric, it will evoke mental comparison with the other architectural orders (Ionic, Corinthian, etc.) which are not in this instance spatially co-present. This relation is associative' (*ibid*: 122). It is this latter which is now more commonly referred to as a paradigmatic relation.

It is tempting to map the syntagmatic/paradigmatic distinction on to that between *langue* and *parole*, seeing syntagmatic relations as typically those of speech and paradigmatic relations as those of the structuring system of *langue*. However, as Saussure points out, although a sentence is definitively a syntagma, syntagmatic relations do not as such belong to the domain of speech. The conventions which are operative in both syntagmatic and paradigmatic relations are elements of *langue* serving to define the nature of permissible sequencing and the array of elements available to the language user. The analytic boundary between *langue* and *parole*, therefore, does not coincide with that between paradigmatic and syntagmatic. Like all Saussure's binary distinctions, that between paradigmatic and syntagmatic is an analytic abstraction designed to simplify and thus comprehend a more complex reality.

There remains one further key distinction in the Saussurian lexicon. Looming over Saussure's entire project is his differentiation between synchronic and diachronic linguistics. It is the former which takes precedence in his work, concerned, as it is, with charting the 'logical and psychological connexions between co-existing items constituting a system, as perceived by the same collective consciousness [*conscience collective*]' (*ibid*: 98). In synchronic linguistics we seek to understand the fundamental workings of *langue*. In diachronic linguistics, by contrast, it is not the character of *langue* itself which is the topic, but the events which change it over time. Such change comes about through speech, or, rather, as a consequence of the freedom which speech has to improvise and imitate in ways that can change usage. By its very nature, for Saussure, this does not constitute a system in the same way that the systematicity of language can be synchronically understood. It is an application of individual agency rather than collective structure, and although Part Three of the *Cours* is devoted to diachronic linguistics, the main emphasis in Saussure's work is on the task of synchronic understanding. Thus, although he does have observations to make on the evolution of language, and on questions of etymology and geographical variation, the primary focus of his theory – as it will be the structuralism that he inspires – is on systematic and scientific comprehension of the state of *langue* at a given moment in whatever semiological system forms the focus. That is Saussure's central goal.

Structuralism and cultural studies

So far, we have isolated the major elements in Saussure's thinking which formed a framework for the development of structuralism and, in turn, deeply influenced cultural studies. The key distinctions between *langue* and *parole*, signifier and signified, paradigmatic and syntagmatic, and synchronic and diachronic, along with his stress on the arbitrary character of the sign and the relational concept of language, come together to form the fundamental terms of semiology – the scientific study of sign-systems. However, as I have already suggested, the initial influence of Saussure's ideas was heavily mediated, filtered through the work of a group of mainly French scholars who extended and amended his theories. In consequence, Saussurian concepts entered cultural studies often disconnected from each other, and given different inflections by different interpreters and translators. Rather than chart the detail of this variation – which would be a very considerable task – I shall first try to draw out some of the general analytic implications of Saussure's ideas, a strategy which will allow me to examine in broad terms the potential that structuralism brought to cultural studies without becoming bogged down in the minutiae of 'structuralist' scholarship. Then, equipped with this abstract and *post hoc* account of structuralism's significance, I shall return to the initial mediation of structuralist ideas by Barthes and Lévi-Strauss with a view to understanding their changing impact in the years that followed.

Inevitably we begin with *langue* and *parole*, since that distinction catches so much of what was important in Saussure's thinking. Imagine the spirit of such a distinction applied not to the domain of linguistics but to cultural artefacts more generally. We saw in Chapter 2 that post-war thought, where it did not simply dismiss whole reaches of modern culture as polluted by their mass origins, tended to focus on the detailed interpretation of the individual 'text'. In literary criticism, in film studies, in art history, the isolated novel, film or painting formed the main focus for critical and interpretive activity. Or, if not entirely the isolated text, then artefacts united by their common authorship, since a presumption that art was authored was also central to established conceptions of culture. Typically within this world view, the critic's task was to expose and appraise the artistry of authorship and the transcendent significance of the artist's creation. In effect, then, the cultural critic took individual instances of 'speech' – particular 'texts' – and subjected them to close analysis with a view to their evaluation and appreciation. What s/he did not do, however, was to ask in any thoroughgoing way about the system, the *langue*, which underwrote their operation. For if these discrete cultural artefacts can indeed be treated as 'speech', then extension of Saussure's ideas suggests that their very realization as communicative experiences depends upon a 'language system' – or, more likely, several interlocking language systems, since novels, films and paintings draw upon varied semiological resources.

So, to map culture directly in terms of the *langue/parole* distinction leads away from the traditional approach, which is primarily concerned to expose the meaning and value of discrete artefacts, and toward a concern with the system(s) which enable those artefacts to have meaning in the first place. A 'structuralist' approach, then, is one which transcends individual texts and, indeed, disciplines. Any texts are grist to the mill for a mode of analysis which primarily seeks to understand the system of codes and conventions through which particular texts are constructed by their creators and understood by their consumers. Accordingly, Saussure's emphasis on *langue* has the potential to redirect cultural studies just as radically as it redirected linguistics, providing a framework within which cultural materials normally considered the province of this or that discipline may be analysed in terms of trans-disciplinary, semiological concepts. Also, of course, it undercuts the familiar commitment to individualism in orthodox cultural criticism, so clearly given expression in the traditional centrality of the author, that figure derided by structuralist critic Roland Barthes (1977a: 146) as the 'Author-God'. It is not necessary to go as far as Barthes in proclaiming 'the death of the author' to appreciate quite how significant a shift it is from celebrating the creative work of authors to analysing the operation of language systems and modelling those systems in abstract terms.

Yet care is required here, since to stress the centrality of *langue* is not necessarily to eliminate human agency among authors and readers, even if, as we shall see, a tendency to 'decentre the subject' prevailed in the first phase of influence of structuralism upon cultural studies. Though Saussurian ideas do orient us toward developing a theory of the operation of language systems rather than toward their users, the ontology underlying his thinking still retains a concept of active agency. *Langue*, it will be recalled, is an enabling system. To think in terms of *langue* and *parole* is to think in terms of speakers and hearers actively using the resources of their shared language system – restricted by codes and conventions in what they are able to express, certainly, but also equipped to combine elements inventively within and because of that conventional framework. Of course it is true that the major structuralist emphasis is on the system and its structuring capacities. However, the model is not one in which the structure *determines* outcomes, but one in which agents are both 'constrained and enabled' (cf. Giddens, 1984) by the language system. Speakers and hearers remain active users of the cultural materials at their disposal.

Now let us add to this account Saussure's conception of the sign, decomposed, as he sees it, into a signifier and a signified which stand in an 'arbitrary' relation to one another. Arbitrary, remember, does not mean random or disordered. It is a way of denying an intrinsic or 'natural' link between signifier and signified, stressing instead the socially conventional and constructed character of signification processes. A text, then, itself composed of a multiplicity of signs, is conventional in its very fabric. Though it might purport to represent a 'real' external world, for example to 'reflect reality', such a representation is always precisely that – a *representation* constructed within the terms provided by the language systems in use. Not only constructed, of course, but also comprehended in terms of those sets of codes and conventions. So, if Saussure's ideas of *langue* and the sign are writ large, they lead us toward a heavily relativized understanding of culture, wherein artefacts must always be understood in relation to the codes utilized in their construction and interpretation.

This has several significant implications for traditional approaches. To begin with, the conventional critical pursuit of a final, 'true' interpretation of a work of art is seen for the illusion that it is. The meaning of a text is not fixed, but depends upon context. Texts become what they are because they are made and read in specific coding environments, in relation to networks of language systems. Language, Saussure tells us, is relational. Its terms take their value from their position in the whole system. In such a relational system there is constant potential for polysemy, as texts are used and understood in variable contexts. The more elaborate the textual form, the more that potential is realised; both as a consequence of the sheer complexity of highly developed language systems and because so many forms of culture draw upon more than one such system. So, while one emphasis within structuralism clearly displaces the social agent in favour of the structuring capacities of language-like systems, another recognizes that in their very functioning those systems open up, rather than close down, potential for variation in meaning and in 'readership'. It is in this sense that so-called post-structuralism – with its emphasis on the indeterminacy of meaning – is rooted deep in the tensions of the original structuralist project.

Those tensions can also be seen at work in applications of the Saussurian syntagmatic/paradigmatic distinction, which proposes two classes of relations among the units from which a semiotic system is constructed. These sequencing and associative relations are, of course, coded by the *langue*: we cannot simply choose which units to use and in what order, at least not if we wish to be understood by those who share our culture with us. But, again, there are considerable degrees of freedom here, and although the first task of a structuralist account may be to identify the units from which a text is composed and thence the codes which govern their arrangement – the goal of synchronic analysis – in application to complex cultural forms, structuralist concepts do not exclude change over time (the diachronic dimension), differential application of codes in different contexts, and different levels of coding.

All of which is no more than to say that the Saussurian inheritance is not entirely unambiguous in the balance it proposes between the constraints of structure and the inventive capacities of agency. Its main thrust is clear enough, to be sure, and is conveyed by Saussure's stress on the paramount importance of synchronically comprehending *langue*. Given this emphasis, the major task of a structuralist analysis in cultural studies would have to be that of modelling the workings of all the various language systems which intersect in forming cultural artefacts. In effect, to extend and develop the project that Saussure sketched for semiology. To do that requires above all the development of theory: identifying the basic units of semiotic systems and building models which embody the codes governing their operation. Such model building, note, differs epistemologically both from the conventional empiricist view of scientific theory, with its atomistic emphasis on hypothesis testing, and from the looser sense of 'theory' found in more literary traditions, where it has tended to suggest a concern to explore basic 'philosophical' assumptions. Structuralist theory, at least as it is implied in Saussure's thinking, fundamentally seeks to model the relational structures that enable agents to involve themselves in processes of communication. Its success is measured not by experimental test or by moral insight, but by the capacity of its models to make sense out of our ways of producing and using cultural forms.

In its main line of development structuralism offered cultural studies both an overarching, trans-disciplinary framework, and a set of concepts which suggested the outlines of a method of analysis. Concern with *langue*, with the coding of signification, with the whole project of semiology, pointed toward an enterprise which could uncover structural fixity in the midst of cultural variation. It was this strand of structuralism that dominated the early years, and with mixed results. On the positive side – and this should not be underestimated – structuralism's concern to examine the underlying and enabling structures of culture provided just the theoretical and methodological focus that cultural studies needed to set it on its way. Without this impetus, it is difficult to imagine the 'discipline' developing as it has. On the negative side, early structuralist cultural studies attracted the charge of excessive formalism which later led to mounting concerns about the drift toward textual determinism. As we shall see, both accusations had some merit. However, in the event, neither was sufficient to undermine the credibility of structuralist perspectives, partly because structuralism itself proved highly adaptable. So-called post-structuralist counter-positions were rapidly derived from those features of Saussure's thought which foregrounded the relational and polysemic character of complex communication. Indeed, the 'post' in post-structuralism may be something of a misnomer, given how dependent such positions are on Saussure's original thinking. I shall return to that in Chapter 4. First it is necessary to pay somewhat closer attention to two of the major contributors to, and mediators of, that first wave of structuralist influence: Claude Lévi-Strauss and Roland Barthes.

The perils of formalism

Edith Kurzweil (1980) calls Lévi-Strauss 'the father of structuralism', and there is no doubt that he, more than anyone, was
responsible for the early promotion of structural analysis as a new
and stimulating approach to the human sciences. His essay
'L'Analyse structurale en linguistique et en anthropologie' (translated as Chapter 2 of Lévi-Strauss, 1972) first appeared in 1945,
and in it he made a case for applying to anthropology the principles
of structural linguistics – the social science, he suggested, 'in
which by far the greatest progress has been made' (*ibid*: 31). As his
thinking developed in the 1950s and 1960s, he produced a body of
work which was clearly marked by the influence of the Saussurian
tradition. The familiar distinctions between paradigmatic and syntagmatic, synchronic and diachronic, *langue* and *parole*, all inform
his thought, everywhere united in an attempt to understand the
relational structure of complex representational systems.

However, his is not a straightforward application of Saussurian
concepts, and Lévi-Strauss offers his own distinctive variation on
structuralist ideas. In particular, he foregrounds two features that
were to become especially significant in the first phase of structuralist influence on cultural studies. Saussure, it will be recalled,
focused upon the underlying system of *langue*, noting that in so
doing he was concerned to distinguish the social and essential
from the individual and ancillary. As we have already seen, for
him the key task was to grasp the 'logical and psychological connexions between co-existing items constituting a system, as
perceived by the same collective consciousness [*conscience collective*]' (Saussure, 1983: 98). The use of the Durkheimian
conscience collective here underscores Saussure's interest in the
system of shared *social* conventions, but a system which was not
consciously perceived by individuals and which had to be

reconstructed by the analyst. In Saussure, notably, this conception is not cast in terms of any distinctive notion of the unconscious. Lévi-Strauss, however, comes to read the structuralist project with a view to apprehending unconscious structures, and to see those structures as universal: 'the unconscious activity of the mind consists in imposing forms upon content, and if these forms are fundamentally the same for all minds – ancient and modern, primitive and civilised' (Lévi-Strauss, 1972: 21). Paradoxically, then, what we see here is a social anthropologist undercutting the strong social and relativistic potential of Saussurian structuralism in favour of an approach which seeks to comprehend underlying structure in terms of universal, unconscious categories – to reveal what an unconvinced Edmund Leach (1970: 60) described as 'a single unitary message inherent in the architecture of the human mind'.

The second distinctive feature of Lévi-Strauss' structuralism derives particularly from his admiration for Jakobson's approach to phonemic analysis. As he does in many of his early writings, Lévi-Strauss turns to kinship to illustrate his point. 'Like phonemes,' he argues (1972: 34), 'kinship terms are elements of meaning; like phonemes, they acquire meaning only if they are integrated into systems. "Kinship systems," like "phonemic systems," are built by the mind on the level of unconscious thought.' Accordingly, he suggests, the systems are of the same type and may be understood using analogous methods. Since Jakobson's method centres upon binary oppositions, it is this binarism on which Lévi-Strauss draws in formulating his own methodology. Where Jakobson worked with oppositions between elements such as vowels and consonants and with contradictions which can be related to each other because they are analogous in form, Lévi-Strauss seeks out permutations and combinations of units in kinship, in totemic systems, and, above all, in myth, where, in a hugely ambitious series of works, he sought to uncover the elements out of which all myths were constructed.

Leavening Saussurian structuralism with a focus on universal, unconscious structures and a method grounded in basic binary distinctions leads Lévi-Strauss to a series of esoteric, complex, and sometimes all but impenetrable works of detailed analysis. At its simplest, this involves taking diverse myths, breaking them into their constituent units – in the early stages he called them 'mythemes' – and trying to show how their combinations and per-mutations, their inversions and transformations, can be understood in terms of fundamental binary oppositions such as those between Life and Death, Nature and Culture, Raw and Cooked. But as he progresses from the basic argument of his famous 1955 essay 'The Structural Study of Myth' (1972: 206–231) through the four vol-umes of *Mythologiques* (1970, 1973, 1978, 1990), it becomes increasingly difficult to accept his ingenious interpretative accounts at face value. As Culler (1975: 47) observes, in the context of a broadly sympathetic critique: 'when, as is so often the case, Lévi-Strauss compares two myths from different cultures and claims to derive their meaning from the relations between them, his analysis may become very problematic indeed. There is no *a priori* reason to think that the myths have anything to do with one another.' No *a priori* reason, that is, other than Lévi-Strauss' con-viction that his method allows him to reveal structures which derive from the basic categories of human thought.

What Lévi-Strauss is doing in his myth analysis is offering com-plex, conjunctive readings of networks of texts with a view to establishing the set of elements of which they are all transforma-tions. The appeal of such a strategy to the youthful cultural studies of the late 1960s and early 1970s will be immediately apparent, especially where popular cultural genres could be directly likened to myths, and for a brief period Lévi-Straussian structuralist

method was seen as the most promising way to extend structuralism into general cultural analysis. Little of this material has
survived the passage of time with any credibility, and where it
has – as in the case of Wright's (1975) study of the Western – it is
often because key modifications were made to the basic Lévi-
Straussian framework. Wright, for example, understands his
structures as reflecting social circumstances rather than fundamental features of the mind, and draws upon other sources, notably
Propp, for his method of narrative analysis.

Nevertheless, Lévi-Strauss' particular realization of structuralist
method did have significant longer-term consequences for cultural
studies. It played an important part in ensuring that the first impact
of structuralism emphasized the distinctively formalist potential of
the approach. A Lévi-Straussian analysis, after all, demanded that
the analyst identified the units from which texts were constructed,
did so largely in isolation from the actual reading practices of consumers of those texts, and arrived at an account of 'meaning' by
examining the formal combinations and permutations of those
units across the (trans-cultural) corpus of texts. Such an approach
is 'formalist' in several senses. First, and most obviously, it focuses
on the formal patterning of cultural materials across the whole set
of artefacts, treating this as revealing the most significant 'meanings' which texts carry. In doing that, however, it abstracts texts
from their culture, reifying revealed form. The texts come to carry
meaning in consequence of the structures that the analysis uncov-
ers, a process which functions quite independently of the social
agents who make and use culture. In other words, both the social
and the individual recede into the background of such an analysis –
the 'forms' themselves provide sufficient grounds for credible
interpretative conclusions. Accordingly, it is difficult to say anything about the social role of cultural forms except at the most
general level – Lévi-Strauss (1972: 224), for instance, proclaims

somewhat extravagantly that 'mythical thought always progresses from the awareness of oppositions toward their resolution' – and the expressive or emotional dimension of culture as it is experienced by individuals is all but unthinkable within this framework. So much so that, in the wake of this kind of formalism, it was to be some years before a structuralist-inspired cultural studies found terms in which to address questions about the expressive pleasures afforded by texts.

Yet the charge of over-formalism should not be laid entirely at Lévi-Strauss' door. The other major figure who influenced the character of early structuralism as it was perceived by cultural studies, Roland Barthes, although significantly less austere in his formalist commitments, also did much to promote a formally inclined mode of semiological analysis. Unlike Lévi-Strauss, however, Barthes' thinking proved more fluid over time, a feature of his work which can be stimulating and frustrating in equal measure. It leads Culler (1990: 9–23) to view him as a 'man of parts', and so he was, constantly pursuing a plurality of interests and several times revising his principal theoretical commitments. Here I shall be concerned primarily with Barthes the systematic semiologist, since it is this aspect of his work which most significantly affected early cultural studies. Roughly speaking, this phase comes to an end in 1973 with the publication of *S/Z* (Barthes, 1990) and is dominated by his writings of the 1950s and 1960s. As this early work was made available to an English-speaking readership, it contributed to a distinctive cultural studies vision of the semiological enterprise.

As with Lévi-Strauss, Barthes' debt to Saussure is both apparent and professed. He begins his 1964 systematization of semiology (Barthes, 1973) with a reference to Saussure's *Cours*, and by the end of his 'Introduction' he has already invoked three of the classic Saussurian distinctions. They serve as organizing principles for his study. However, also like Lévi-Strauss, he develops his own reading of Saussure as well as drawing upon subsequent work in linguistics and elsewhere, work by the likes of Hjelmslev, Jakobson, Lacan, and Lévi-Strauss himself. Indeed, Barthes' revisionism goes so far as to claim that Saussure may have been mistaken in viewing linguistics as but one application of the general science of semiology; instead Barthes proposes that semiology should be understood as a part of linguistics. But however tenable that inversion may seem – and it hangs upon an assumption about the pervasiveness of ordinary language and the concomitant need for a 'trans-linguistics' – Barthes, at this stage at least, remains committed to the classical semiological project. 'The aim of semiological research,' he writes, 'is to reconstitute the functioning of the systems of significations other than language in accordance with the process typical of any structuralist activity, which is to build a *simulacrum* of the object under observation' (Barthes, 1973: 95). Accordingly, when in 1966 he comes to examine narrative (Barthes, 1977b), it is with a view to modelling the *langue* of narrativity from which specific narratives may be generated.

His work on narrative, along with that of other French 'narratologists' such as Bremond, Genette, Greimas and Todorov, was crucial in stimulating a growing interest in the subject within cultural studies. Narratives, after all, are ubiquitous in modern cultures, so to uncover a *langue* of narrativity would indeed be a major achievement. Later, and with characteristic iconoclasm, Barthes would mock the somewhat grandiose scientific ambitions of these early semiological projects, but at the time it was precisely that aspiration which made the semiology of narrative so appealing. The very formalism of narrative analysis (an approach derived also from the work of the Russian Formalists) made it seem scientifically credible and gave impetus to the kind of detailed examination of narrative conventions which thus far had not characterized Anglo-American perspectives on culture. Just by making narrative into a distinct topic of study in itself, Barthes and the French narratologists did a considerable service to the youthful enterprise of cultural studies.

However, Barthes' early approach to narrative was not the central innovation of his semiological work, nor the locus of his major influence. That honour should perhaps be accorded to his addition of the denotative/connotative distinction to the standard armoury of structuralist concepts. Barthes was not the originator of that distinction – he develops it from Hjelmslev, surely the biggest influence on his semiology after Saussure – but it is a constant undercurrent in his earliest essays. It is this distinction which he formalizes as the fourth organizing principle of *Elements of Semiology*, adding it to the Saussurian trio of *langue/parole*, signifier/signified and syntagmatic/associative, and it is this distinction, therefore, that we must examine if we are to understand Barthes' theoretical and methodological impact on early cultural studies. What, then, is at the root of his insistence on distinguishing between denotation and connotation?

We can begin to see what is at issue by looking at his discussion (Barthes, 1977c) of the 'photographic paradox', the fact that, at first sight at least, the photographic image appears semiologically misbegotten – 'a message without a code'. Generally, he suggests, the photographic image is viewed not as a transformation of its object through coded signification, but as standing in an analogical relation to it. In other apparently analogical forms (Barthes includes paintings, drawings, theatre and cinema) there is a second level of meaning generated by the way in which the representation is treated (its 'style') which, in the context of a particular culture, itself carries a message. Such forms as these, then, 'comprise two messages: a *denoted* message, which is the *analogon* itself, and a *connoted* message, which is the manner in which the society to a certain extent communicates what it thinks of it' (*ibid*: 17). The connoted message is certainly coded, understood through the filters of our various symbolic orders. So we *see* the replication of reality denoted by the image, but we *understand* connotative meanings in consequence of the interaction of that image with cultural codes. Yet photography commonly presents itself as a 'mechanical analogue' without a second-order message; a newspaper photograph, for example, is pure denotation. Or is it?

Barthes' suggestion is that the claim of photographs to the denotative, to 'objectivity', is misleading: a naturalized product of 'common sense'. In the act of reading a photograph we relate it to a body of signs, and it is in this process that what begins as a message without a code is assimilated by its readers to a connotative system. 'Connotation, the imposition of second meaning on the photographic message proper, is realized at the different levels of production of the photograph (choice, technical treatment, framing, lay-out) and represents, finally, a coding of the photographic analogue' (*ibid*: 20). How this is managed is, for Barthes, a central question for semiology, and one with which he had been grappling for some years. Hence, of course, the famous example from his first (1957) attempt to think through his views, at this stage without use of the terms denotation and connotation. Let me quote it at length, since it so clearly embodies his central concerns.

On the cover [of *Paris-Match*], a young Negro in a French uniform is saluting, with his eyes uplifted, probably fixed on a fold of the tricolour. All this is the *meaning* of the picture. But, whether naively or not, I see very well what it signifies to me: that France is a great Empire, that all her sons, without any colour discrimination, faithfully serve under her flag, and that there is no better answer to the detractors of an alleged colonialism than the zeal shown by this Negro in serving his so-called oppressors. I am therefore again faced with a greater semiological system: there is a signifier, itself already formed with a previous system (*a black soldier is giving the French salute*); there is a signified (it is here a purposeful mixture of

Frenchness and militariness); finally, there is a presence of the signified through the signifier. (Barthes, 1993: 116)

At this early stage Barthes was examining the process under the
rubric of *myth*; his example is offered as an instance of 'mythical
speech'. But the essence of his account is that there are two systems of signification at work here whereby the sign of the primary
system (the photograph of the soldier) becomes the signifier of the
secondary, or mythical, system. In the essays collected in
Mythologies it is this 'second-order semiological system' that forms
Barthes' focus – the metalanguage, as he then calls it, through
which first-order signification comes to carry specific, naturalized
meanings. In 'Myth Today' (Barthes, 1993: 109–159) he begins to
try abstractly to formulate that relationship, and later, in *Elements
of Semiology*, to extend his formal account in terms of the concepts
of denotation and connotation.

This leads him to untangle two features of second-order systems that are conflated in his earlier discussions. Imagine that, as
in Barthes' earlier example, we have two systems of signification,
S_1 and S_2, in which the former is an element of the latter. Given
that each is composed of signifiers and signifieds (or, in the terms
Barthes borrows from Hjelmslev, each comprises a plane of
expression and a plane of content) it is necessary to distinguish
two forms of relation between them. S_1 may be the signifier of the
second system, its plane of expression, in which case we are confronted with a plane of denotation (S_1) and a plane of connotation
(S_2). Most commonly, Barthes suggests, this is to be found where
natural language forms S_1 and, mounted on it, so to speak, we find
a second, wider connotative system (S_2), as is the case with literature. But the same reasoning applies to Barthes' discussions of
photography or to his analysis of the *Paris-Match* cover, where
one system is taken as the denotative foundation for a broader

connotative or inferential apparatus. This, following Hjelmslev, is the domain of connotative semiotics, and Barthes (1973: 90) observes, with the period's characteristic optimism, that 'the future probably belongs to a linguistics of connotation'. However, what if S_1 is not the signifier of S_2 – its plane of expression – but its signified, or plane of content? In this case, S_2 becomes a metalanguage which has S_1 as its language object – the relation found between, among others, semiology and the significatory systems that it analyses. It follows, of course, that each metalanguage could become the plane of content for yet another secondary system, and so on up a scale of encompassing metalanguages.

What are the consequences of this somewhat confusing analysis? On the question of connotation, what is clear is that not only does Barthes see connotative semiotics as central to the future of semiology, but he also considers this form of analysis to raise directly the question of ideology: '[a]s for the signified of connotation, its character is at once general, global and diffuse; it is, if you like, a fragment of ideology' (*ibid*: 91). The signified of connotation is ideology, while its signifiers are constituted by the rhetorics which convert the denotation of S_1 into the connoted meanings of S_2. Subjected to the appropriate rhetorics, the soldier saluting the flag comes to signify the ideology of French militaristic imperialism. Meanwhile, the semiologist, who is marshalling a different S_2 in the cause of metalanguage analysis, is both obliged thereby to untangle the web from which connotation is constructed and to recognize that, in turn, this very semiological account may itself be relativized within further metalanguages. So, Barthes concludes (*ibid*: 94), the semiologist 'seems to have the objective function of decipherer . . . in relation to the world which naturalizes or conceals the signs of the first system under the signifiers of the second; but his objectivity is made provisional by the very history which renews metalanguages'. The general task of semiology may quite properly be rendered in terms of modelling all the many systems of signification which surround us, but its more specific realization for Barthes involves a qualified demystification of the naturalized, connotative meanings which are the essence of ideology.

In this early stage of Barthes' work, then, he extends the structuralist project in two (perhaps incompatible) directions, one of which is founded in orthodox, semiological formalism, while the other is concerned primarily with connotative semiotics. The first is epitomized in his pre-*S/Z* approach to narrative, with its deductive concern to model the *langue* of narrativity, identifying narrative units, functions and actions along the way, all of which played a significant part in establishing narrative as a key concern of cultural studies. This project would be recognized by any reader of Saussure as a straightforward extension of basic structuralism, akin to, though by no means identical with, Lévi-Strauss' desire to model the structure of myth. It is also this formal emphasis on the power of *langue* that leads to the displacement of the authorial subject – the rhetoric of 'the death of the author'. 'It is language which speaks,' Barthes writes, 'not the author' (Barthes, 1977a: 143), an invocation which, for all its sacrifice of authorial agency to linguistic structure, did at least serve to remind literary-based cultural studies of the pervasive dangers of author-centred, intentionalist analyses of texts.

The second thread of argument is less straightforward, but certainly more original and, in the end, probably more significant. In attending so determinedly to connotative semiotics, whether under that rubric itself or, as it was initially, in the myth analysis of *Mythologies*, Barthes contributed to the formation of several subsequent motifs in cultural studies. Though he was not solely responsible for it, he played his part in yoking together the concepts of signification, naturalization and ideology, and although the latter term remained descriptive and under-theorized in his work, that was a deficiency for which later structuralists would more than compensate. The problem of formulating an appropriate theory of ideology was to dominate cultural studies for many years to come. His concern with connotation also led him to begin to formulate the role of cultural codes in the workings of semiotic systems, a feature which is apparent in his study of fashion (Barthes, 1983) and in the rather different concept of code deployed in *S/Z*, where, he says, *contra* orthodox semiology, he is 'concerned not to manifest a structure but to produce a structuration' (Barthes, 1990: 20). The idea of code, too, was to play an important role in subsequent cultural studies, though not always with the processual emphasis that Barthes seems to intend here. And lastly, in parallel with his displacement of authorship, he begins to envisage the reading of texts more positively than in much early structuralism, postulating a reader who is 'no longer a consumer, but a producer of the text' (*ibid*: 4), who is already caught up in a plurality of texts and codes, and for whom reading is work, 'a labour of language' (*ibid*: 10–11). But by then, of course, Barthes – the 'man of parts' – is no longer the formal semiologist of his early years, and his structuralism is edging toward what will come to be thought of as post-structuralism.

Barthes and Lévi-Strauss bend structuralism (and hence early cultural studies) in distinctive directions, not always consistent with each other and, in Barthes' case, changing significantly over time. Their motifs, the theoretical and methodological topics that they emphasize, include formal analysis of texts, a concern with unconscious structures, systematic binarism, a desire to decode *langue* in multiple contexts, myth analysis, connotative semiotics, deciphering naturalized messages of ideology, and displacing the subject, all of which feature in the first flowering of structuralist cultural studies. And their characteristic omissions – a fully theorized sense of the social functioning of cultural texts, a coherent grasp of the operation of agency and subjectivity in cultural production and consumption, a conceptualization of the pleasures afforded by culture – come to be seen as problems of structuralism *per se* rather than of their particular inflection of it. The term which, however inadequately, was increasingly used to express these doubts about the first wave of structuralist work was 'formalism', and in the 1970s various schools of thought within cultural studies tried to reformulate their structuralist foundations in such a way as to counter that charge. In Chapters 4 and 5 we shall examine some of the terms of this reformulation. But however vigorously later scholars may claim to transcend structuralism – and some have been very loud in their protestations – the intellectual foundation provided by Saussure, and subsequently developed by Barthes and Lévi-Strauss, remains the single most profound source of theory and method in cultural studies. Without structuralism, cultural studies as we now understand it is all but inconceivable.

4 *Situating Subjects*

The passage that we must now negotiate is that from structuralism to post-structuralism. It is not a passage through clear, calm seas, nor are its ports of embarkation and destination precisely mapped. Although Chapter 3 has given us some sense of the topography of Saussurian structuralism, as we also saw in that chapter Saussure's French interpreters soon began to extend his principles in unexpected directions. Quite when they crossed the line into 'post-structuralism' is unclear, so much so that I am tempted not to use the expression at all without the ironic protection afforded by quotation marks. Post-structuralism is an all too elastic concept. Rather like the famous post-Impressionist exhibition once mounted in London's Royal Academy and, to this bemused spectator at least, seemingly composed of every style of painting after 1905, post-structuralism expands without limit to encompass vast reaches of European thought. Whereas most would agree that Derrida is post-structuralist, or Kristeva, or Barthes after *S/Z*, some might balk at Foucault, or throw up their hands at that prophet of the postmodern, Lyotard. Indeed, more confusion has been sown by that simple prefix 'post' than by any number of muddled attempts to define structuralism in the first place.

Yet we must have limits, and for my purposes post-structuralism begins at just that point when structuralists turn away from the classic semiological project. Barthes, with whom the last chapter ended, offers as good a symptomology as any. In *Elements of Semiology*, and in the work surrounding it, he is concerned to establish the concepts necessary to explore the underlying language systems of different forms of signification: Saussure's enterprise of semiology. But with *S/Z* that project changes. Barthes' interest in narrative is no longer focused on extracting the master narrative structure, because to do so is to deny 'difference' and 'plurality' within the text and thereby to fail to grasp the productivity of reading. Even classical narratives, 'readerly' texts (as opposed to 'writerly') which limit the freedom of the reader to be 'no longer a consumer, but a producer of the text' (Barthes, 1990: 4), even such texts display at least a partial plurality. So, Barthes takes Balzac's story '*Sarrasine*' and subjects it to a microscopic analysis with a view to grasping its multiplicity. To describe this attack on the text he uses expressions like 'manhandling' and 'interrupting', collapsing it into lexias (fragments of various lengths that are his units of reading) and examining them using five categories of code. But this does not invoke the socially grounded conventions of classical semiology, a formal mechanism regulating signification: 'we use *Code* here not in the sense of a list, a paradigm that must be reconstituted. The code is a perspective of quotations, a mirage of structures' (*ibid*: 20). Examining in rich detail the play of difference in the text, Barthes seeks to produce what he calls a 'structuration', an understanding of reading-in-process rather than an account of underlying structure.

Here, then, we see the early steps in a move away from classical structuralism. First, the individual text has edged nearer to the centre of things, no longer one instance among many to be placed and understood formally within the system of a *langue*, but a field of possibilities to be excavated in terms of a fluid network of codes. Secondly, the reader, or, rather, the process of readership, takes its place at the conceptual heart of the enterprise. I stress 'readership' here because the term 'reader' already hypostasizes a subject, an 'I' outside the text, and it is against such fixed ideas of subjectivity that Barthes and other 'post-structuralists' counterpose their views. Thirdly, the attribution of meaning is seen as a constant process of (re)construction among the play of signifiers, texts endlessly open to a plurality of readings and re-readings, none of them privileged as first or last. Text, subject, plurality: in these three we see both a denial and an extension of structuralism. A denial in the sense of discarding the semiological project, the goal of uncovering an underlying formal system which mechanistically enables social agents to use and understand signs. An extension in as much as texts, subjects and their conjoint plurality are constituted within the conceptual field of those earlier structuralist perspectives. In that respect, these are indeed post-structuralist texts and subjects.

How does this move manifest itself in cultural studies? Unevenly, certainly, and in the first instance very much within the field of film theory. We saw in Chapter 2 how film became a focus for those especially concerned to develop a different approach to popular culture to that found in traditional mass culture perspectives. Unsurprisingly, then, it was in relation to the task of theorizing film 'language' that first semiology and then various post-structuralist innovations entered the English-speaking world of cultural studies. Peter Wollen (1969a, 1969b) played an important part in this development, both in his own writings and in his influence upon the emergence of the journal *Screen* as a crucial locus for theoretical debate. For much of the 1970s – but especially during the first five years – *Screen* served as a channel through which the latest (post-)structuralist thinking was brought to the attention of British and American film scholarship. Not only that, *Screen* also began to forge its own distinctive synthesis of structuralism, Althusserian marxism and Lacanian psychoanalytic theory – a heady mixture which was to set the terms of film theoretical discussion for years to come (for a good account see Jancovich, 1995). Later, members of the Birmingham Centre for Contemporary Cultural Studies (see Chapter 5) would label these views '*Screen* theory', and I shall borrow their usage here. It is to *Screen* theory that we must turn our attention if we are to trace the impact of structuralism any further.

Making *Screen* theory 1: semiotics and psychoanalysis

All that appeared in *Screen* did not, of course, play a part in *Screen* theory, so it is important to remember that the account I shall offer here is abstracted from a much wider corpus of work. Contributors (including the present author) were often in disagreement with each other, sometimes violently, although it is true to say that by the mid-1970s a distinctive line of argument and, therefore, a kind of collective intellectual identity could be ascribed to the journal. *Screen* had developed a 'problematic', to borrow a favoured Althusserian term. Many traditions contributed to this synthesis, including, among those to which I shall not attend, Brechtian theory, Russian Formalism, and a range of arguments about realism and avant-gardism in several artistic contexts. Since my aim here is to characterize the main thrust of *Screen* theory as that was to influence subsequent cultural studies thinking, I shall look only at a key triangle of concerns: film semiotics; ideology; and the subject.

On film semiotics it is instructive to consider the broad trajectory of Christian Metz' work, partly because Metz featured prominently both in translation and as a topic for discussion in the pages of *Screen* (see, in particular, *Screen*, 14, 1/2, 1973; 14, 3, 1973; 16, 2, 1975) and partly because the movement of his thought embodies some of the same shifts apparent in *Screen* theory. Roughly speaking, his semiotics of film falls into three phases, here referenced in relation to the English translations in collected form rather than the original essays: a first period in the early to mid-1960s (Metz, 1974a) when he is much exercised by the 'problem' of film's status as a language without a *langue*; a second period culminating in the publication of *Langage et cinéma* in 1971 (Metz, 1974b) in which those earlier reservations are left behind in a systematic attempt to examine the units, codes and language system of cinema; and a third period beginning in the mid-1970s (Metz, 1982) in which the semiotic project is recast in terms of a psychoanalytic attempt to conceptualize the cinematic apparatus. I shall briefly examine the characteristic features of each of those phases, my account of the first two deriving from the rather longer discussion in Tudor (1980).

In his early essays Metz adopts a similar position to that advanced by Barthes (1977c) in relation to photography. In what senses, he asks, can we talk about film as a 'language'? For us to develop a genuine semiology of film we must be able to think in terms of a cinematic *langue* that provides the basis for intelligible film *parole*. But, Metz argues, film cannot meet the criteria that would allow us to accept it as a fully fledged language complete with such a language system. To see it as thus systematized is, perhaps understandably, to be misled by appearances: 'film is too obviously a message for one not to assume that it is coded' (Metz, 1974a: 40). The problem is that film does exhibit certain 'syntactical procedures' which, as a result of frequent use, appear to be aspects of a language system. But that is an illusion. It is not such procedures that allow us to understand the stories that the movies tell us; it is the fact that the movies tell us stories that enables us to learn to understand these procedures.

Because the relation between signifier and signified in the film sign is analogical rather than arbitrary, Metz believes that it makes no sense to think in terms of a distinctive film *langue*. Comprehending a film image is not a matter of social convention, as it should be if Saussurian concepts are to be used. Film has, Metz argues, no 'second articulation', no identifiable units equivalent to the phonemes of linguistics. The shot is not, as some have claimed, the equivalent of a word – if anything it resembles a sentence. The film image is itself the film's speech, and there is not a limited lexicon of images as there is a limited lexicon of words. Taken together, these and others of Metz' arguments in his early essays would appear to render cinesemiotics a dubious prospect, for if we once accept that cinema does not have a *langue* then what is there for the semiologist to study?

We have already had a clue to Metz' answer to this question in his claim that we understand film's 'syntactical procedures' because we have first understood narrative. If this is indeed the case – that it is primarily in relation to narrative that movie syntax has developed – then it is on this that semiotics must focus. But, even in this rather more limited sphere, the endeavour remains fragile: 'Filmic narrativity . . . by becoming stable through convention and repetition over innumerable films, has gradually shaped itself into forms that are more or less fixed, but certainly not immutable' (*ibid*: 101). In short, Metz can find no distinctive film language outside of those procedures relating to narrativity, and so it is that he comes to focus attention not on *langue* but on the analysis of syntagmatic sequencing in narrative film. This is his influential *grande syntagmatique* (*ibid*: 119–146).

Note that there is a kind of un-Saussurian essentialism apparent in Metz' discussion here, a desire to focus upon the uniquely distinctive features of film. This arises in part from his background in Bazinian film aesthetics, and it haunts all three phases of his work. In this early period he is inclined to argue that film is inherently thus-and-thus and that, in consequence, cinesemiotics is restricted in specific ways. In the second phase of his work, however, this essentialist commitment recedes far enough to allow him to embrace a rather different role for the semiologist. Now the analyst's task is to construct codes which will make sense out of what we know about filmic communication. A code, he writes (Metz, 1974b: 101), 'functions at a given moment of its historical evolution as a closed system which regulates choices which can be listed, and which permits syntagmatic combinations which can themselves be enumerated'. Inevitably, such codes are in complex interaction with others, and it is in the intersection of all the many codes applying to a text that the 'pluricodic' uniqueness of that particular text is found. In general, then, a code is (1) a construct of (2) a system which (3) explains the ways in which the elements of the text(s) interrelate. To understand the codes that govern 'film language' is therefore to understand the underlying order that makes filmic communication possible, even though that project is no longer cast in terms of a traditional concept of *langue*. The ultimate aim, Metz says, is a formal model of each code, though he suggests that such an achievement may still be very distant. A code is, however, always a 'logical entity' intended by the analyst (who constructs it) to 'explicate and elucidate' the workings of the relevant text(s). A specific film cannot be reduced to such codes; it is created from an unpredictable conjunction of the available coded practices.

In *Langage et cinéma* Metz goes on to elaborate at great length upon a range of codes and sub-codes, paying particular attention to what he calls 'cinematic specificity'. It is here that his earlier concern with the essence of the cinematic image returns in a new guise, appearing, as Heath (1973: 25) puts it in a contemporary commentary in *Screen*, 'to be the point of a certain, potentially damaging, fixation, to acquire even a certain mythical quality, to appeal to something like an "essence" of film'. Yet cinematic codes are always bound up with more general cultural codes, so while cinema clearly cannot be reduced to non-cinematic cultural codes, neither should the study of film signification restrict itself to those aspects unique to cinema itself. To do so is likely to obstruct our understanding, since it is in the continuing interaction between more general codes and the specifically cinematic that we can begin to uncover the mechanisms by which audiences are able to arrive at their empirically variable 'readings' of specific film texts. But in focusing as much as he does on 'cinematic specificity' – and notwithstanding his constructive emphasis on the pluricodic character of texts – Metz develops a fundamentally unsocial conception of cinematic language, one from which the 'reader' and the reader's social world are peculiarly absent.

As we saw in the last chapter, that kind of formalism was typical of structuralism more generally at this stage in its development. As the 1970s progressed, however, there was a growing recognition that additional concepts were required if semiology was to be adequate to the task of understanding diverse systems of signification, concepts which would relocate the enterprise in the social context which had been so important to Saussure himself. Accordingly, in the third phase of his work, Metz (1982: 7) begins to address this requirement, albeit somewhat tangentially. 'The cinematic institution is not just the cinema industry . . . it is also the mental machinery – another industry – which spectators "accustomed to the cinema" have internalised historically and which has adapted them to the consumption of films. (The institution is outside us and inside us, indistinctly collective and intimate, sociological and psychoanalytic . . .).' 'The Imaginary Signifier', the essay from which this quotation is taken, first appeared in English in *Screen* (Metz, 1975) and was to prove a significant step in the journal's movement toward a theory and method of analysis utilizing psychoanalytic concepts.

In this essay Metz addresses the question, 'what contribution can Freudian psychoanalysis make to the study of the cinematic signifier?' (Metz, 1982: 17). Whilst recognizing a number of different possibilities (notably films treated as 'symptoms' of the neuroses of their makers, psychoanalysis of what he calls the 'film script', and psychoanalysis of specific textual systems) his major concern is with developing a psychoanalytic approach not to individual films but to the cinematic signifier itself: 'a direct examination, outside any particular film, of the psychoanalytic implications of the *cinematic*' (*ibid*: 36). Once more, then, he returns to his familiar fascination with the uniquely cinematic features of film. To do so he leans on a number of concepts drawn from Lacan's 'structuralist' revision of Freudian theory, as well as on Freud's own work, using resemblances and parallels between the film spectator's situation and that of the psychoanalytic 'subject' to tease out what he considers to be fundamental features of cinema.

The major psychoanalytic resources on which he draws in his examination of cinematic perception are Lacan's account of the 'mirror stage' and the more general emphasis on Oedipal relations in Freudian and Lacanian theory. But, employing a methodological strategy which will later become common in psychoanalytically disposed film theory, he does not apply these ideas directly, using them, rather, to draw parallels and make metaphoric comparisons. So, for instance, presupposing the utility of Lacan's mirror stage concepts (and, indeed, our familiarity with them) he likens film to a – *the* – mirror. 'Thus film is like the mirror. But it differs from the primordial mirror in one essential point: although, as in the latter, everything may come to be projected, there is one thing and one thing only that is never reflected in it: the spectator's own body' (*ibid*: 45). In the Lacanian mirror stage the child's (mis)recognition of its own body in the mirror gives rise to a unified sense of self, a differentiation of the ego, and ultimately facilitates entry into the Symbolic which is the world of the Law and language. The child identifies with its like in the mirror. But, Metz asks of the film 'mirror', where is the spectator's ego in relation to the cinematic signifier? With what does the spectator identify? He offers two interlinked solutions to this puzzle. At one level, he suggests somewhat obscurely, the spectator identifies 'with himself as a pure act of perception (as wakefulness, alertness): as the condition of possibility of the perceived and hence as a kind of transcendental subject, which comes before every *there is*' (*ibid*: 49). This is primary cinematic identification, identification with one's own 'look'. In fiction films, in addition, he suggests that there is a secondary cinematic identification: that with characters and through the looks of characters within and outside the frame.

This stress on perception (the cinema, he says, is 'more perceptual' than many forms of expression) is then extended into a concern with voyeurism (scopophilia) in an account of what he calls 'the scopic regime of the cinema' (*ibid*: 61). This is again established via a series of resemblance claims, the distinctive character of which is caught in the following passage:

> For its spectator the film unfolds in that simultaneously very close and definitively inaccessible 'elsewhere' in which the child *sees* the amorous play of the parental couple, who are similarly ignorant of it and leave it alone, a pure onlooker whose participation is inconceivable. In this respect the cinematic signifier is not only 'psychoanalytic'; it is more precisely Oedipal in type. (*ibid*: 64)

There is a typical slide here (film – inaccessible 'elsewhere' – seeing amorous play of parental couple – Oedipal – film) in which what begins as a loose description of the film spectator's situation slips into psychoanalytic language, but without it being made clear quite what kind of connection is envisaged. Thus, the cinematic signifier is diagnosed as *precisely* Oedipal' on the least precise of metaphorical grounds – or so it would appear to a reader not already committed to the view that the cinematic situation somehow recreates, feeds off, or resonates with the Oedipal in us all.

Metz, then, in 'The Imaginary Signifier' and in his other writing of this period, moves from a position of (modified) semiotic formalism to one in which psychoanalytic terms are used to unpick the basic cinematic situation of spectatorship. Like many who followed post-structuralism along this road, he does so in the belief that psychoanalysis provides privileged access to subjectivity and, thereby, to cinema's workings as a social institution, even though the 'social' here is understood only in very general psychoanalytic terms, and any sense of social *activity* or agency is entirely lost. *Screen*, too, embraced such a strategy, partly influenced by Metz' formulation, but also arising out of the journal's commitment to a broadly marxist orientation to social and political analysis. This also led toward psychoanalytic concepts, but this time via the concept of ideology as that had been adumbrated by the marxist philosopher Louis Althusser.

Making *Screen* theory 2: ideology and the subject

Althusser's work had begun to attract attention from English scholars in the late 1960s, apparently offering a systematic development of marxist thinking which countered the then prominent traditions of 'humanistic' marxism. The post-war era had seen marxism reread and recast in the light of Marx's early writings, notably the newly translated *Economic and Philosophic Manuscripts of 1844*.

Against this tendency Althusser argued that there was an epistemological break in Marx's work, separating the youthful philosophical speculations from the mature, anti-essentialist science of his 'theoretical anti-humanism' (Althusser, 1969: 227–231). In the course of establishing his reading of Marx, Althusser contributed significantly to a wide range of issues in marxist theory. However, it was his distinctive epistemology and his theory of ideology that most strongly influenced both *Screen* theory and 1970s cultural studies more generally, and it is on these elements of his work that I shall focus here.

Let me begin with epistemology. The twin pillars of Althusser's view of knowledge are his thoroughgoing anti-empiricism and, allied to it, his commitment to the view that a science's object of inquiry is always theoretically constituted. This can best be understood in relation to what he calls 'theoretical practice'. 'Scientific' theoretical practice, as opposed to 'ideological' theoretical practice, is a process of production whereby 'raw material' is transformed into knowledge. However, this is not (as in empiricism) a process whereby 'facts' are persuaded to give up their essence, because the raw material upon which science works is always conceptual and the transformation is therefore from one kind of concept to another. When a science is first constituted, Althusser (1969: 184) writes, it 'does not "work" on a purely objective "given", that of pure and absolute "facts". On the contrary, its particular labour consists of *elaborating its own scientific facts* through a critique of the *ideological "facts"* elaborated by an earlier ideological theoretical practice.' Even when it is fully constituted, science still 'works' on concepts, though now they may be ideological as before, or 'facts' within the terms of the scientific theoretical practice, or concepts from an earlier phase of the science. In his distinctive (and revealing) language, the process is one whereby Generality II works on Generality I to produce

Generality III: one order of concept working upon another, to produce yet a third.

Any reader familiar with twentieth-century theories of knowledge and science will recognize a strong conventionalist element in this formulation. Although Althusser surely believes that there is a 'real' material world, his account of knowledge production operates entirely at the conceptual level. In the course of a forceful critique both of Althusser's epistemology and of its influence upon cultural studies, Lovell (1980) argues that the concept of the 'real-concrete' through which he seeks to sustain a sense of real world reference does not fulfil that task. Instead, he leaves us with a view of knowledge which operates within a hermetically sealed conceptual box, a body of theory (a 'theoretical practice') which constitutes its own object of study and develops its own distinctive 'problematic'. Although it is not a step that Althusser himself takes, it is not far from such a conception to the kind of view espoused by Hindess and Hirst (1977: 19–20) when they go beyond Althusser and suggest that 'what is specified in theoretical discourse can only be conceived through that discourse . . . the entities discourse refers to are constituted in and by it'.

I am not suggesting here that the detail of Althusser's formulation of epistemology entered cultural studies or *Screen* theory in unadulterated form. In fact, there was (and is) relatively little detailed discussion of questions of epistemology and method in this area. What I do want to suggest, however, is that the warrant it gave for theorizing independent of any clear criteria of empirical relevance fed an already incipient theoreticism. For Althusser himself empiricism had a specific meaning in the context of various idealist and essentialist philosophical traditions. In *Screen* theory's use of it, however, empiricism covered an even larger multitude of sins, not the least of which was any claim to be concerned with an empirical domain against which theory might be assessed. Theory becomes, as it were, its own arbiter; a 'theoretical practice' sufficient unto itself. This understanding of theoretical activity as all-embracing marked *Screen* theory in the 1970s and has continued to (mis)inform the use of theory in cultural studies to this day.

In this context, let us turn to Althusser's account of ideology, a reformulation of the marxist concept which was to prove timely in meeting *Screen* theory's need to add a further social dimension to its semiotics of film. Twentieth-century marxism had been increasingly concerned to understand the limits of economic determinism (the 'base', forces of production, relations of production) and the concomitant importance of the 'superstructure' (the state, legal, political and ideological forms). In this Althusser was no exception, developing a complex account of the interrelations of these elements in terms of 'overdetermination' and the 'relative autonomy' of superstructures. He calls for a 'theory of the specific effectivity of the superstructures' (Althusser, 1969: 114), noting that only Gramsci had really tried to develop marxist thinking in this respect, and in his much-quoted 1970 essay 'Ideology and Ideological State Apparatuses' (Althusser, 1977: 123–173) he begins to develop that project. This involves identifying a number of Ideological State Apparatuses (ISAs), additional to the more familiar Repressive State Apparatus, in such areas as religion, education, the family, communications, and culture. The basic difference between the two is simple enough: 'the Repressive State Apparatus functions "by violence", whereas the Ideological State Apparatuses *function "by ideology"*' (*ibid*: 138). But what is ideology?

Althusser's theory of ideology is distinctive first of all in that it is primarily a theory of ideology in general rather than of the specific ideologies which are realised in the ISAs. Conventional accounts of ideology (both marxist and non-marxist) often focus upon distortion, viewing ideology as a departure from truth, as something which can be, even must be, transcended. Althusser's conception is much more comprehensive in the social function that it affords to ideology, so much so that, for him, social life is inconceivable without it. Even before his 'ideological state apparatus' essay he was making such substantial claims: 'ideology (as a system of mass representations) is indispensable in any society if men are to be formed, transformed and equipped to respond to the demands of their conditions of existence' (Althusser, 1969: 235). He grounds his account in two basic propositions. Ideology, he says (Althusser, 1977: 153) 'represents the imaginary relationship of individuals to their real conditions of existence' and, secondly, 'ideology has a material existence' (*ibid*: 155), it exists not in some ideational domain but in social practices and apparatuses. An individual caught within ideology lives it out through the practices which give it material form. S/he is rendered a 'subject' in and through those practices which articulate his/her imaginary relationship with real conditions.

This is the heart of Althusser's theory: 'all ideology has the function (which defines it) of "constituting" concrete individuals as subjects' (*ibid*: 160). In other words, the fundamental category through which human beings are incorporated within ideology is that of the subject. Although it may seem obvious to us that we are individuals with a certain kind of identity, it is precisely this transparency which is so important to the operation of ideology. 'It is indeed a peculiarity of ideology that it imposes (without appearing to do so, since these are "obviousnesses") obviousnesses as obviousnesses, which we cannot *fail to recognize* and before which we have the inevitable and natural reaction of crying out (aloud or in the "still, small voice of conscience"): "That's obvious! That's right! That's true!"' (*ibid*: 161). Recognition of ourselves as subjects, however, is a product not of a natural state of being (identity, soul, personality, or what have you) but of ideology, and Althusser uses the term 'interpellation' to describe the process whereby ideology turns individuals into specific kinds of subjects. Ideology, as it were, summons individuals, 'hails' them, as he also puts it, situates them as seemingly natural subjects of a certain kind. Nor is there any existence outside of this process for, to use another of Althusser's key phrases, we are 'always-already' subjects. There is no escape from interpellation and ideology.

This, then, is very much an account of ideology-in-general, so much so that it would not be unreasonable to conclude that this concept of ideology more or less equates to a generalized concept of culture. Two features, perhaps, militate against such a conclusion. First, Althusser does believe that in 'science' it is possible to find a subjectless discourse, to escape ideology, and secondly, ideology still constitutes an *imaginary* relationship of people to their *real* circumstances. These views (however difficult it would be to sustain the former) ensure that Althusser's concept retains a critical edge which would not necessarily be present in a descriptive concept of culture, provoking analysis which unpacks the illusions of subject positioning through which the real circumstances of people's lives are mediated. The implication for cultural studies is clear. In as much as the fundamental ideological operation is that of constituting subjects, then the first and vital moment of cultural analysis must be that which shows how specific forms perform interpellation. What is the nature of subject formation in, for example, the classic realist text (MacCabe, 1974)? And is it possible (as *Screen* theory was inclined to argue) to produce texts and readings of texts which foreground and undermine these processes of subject formation? The former leads to an avant-garde aesthetic practice; the latter to an approach to 'reading' which seeks out the fractures in the text itself, the slips, the points of subversion of the ideological project.

In this way a congruence is established in *Screen* theory between the Althusserian account of ideology and other of *Screen*'s influences of the period, most notably Brecht, Barthes' intensive reading strategy in *S/Z*, and, influenced by Barthes and psychoanalysis, the much-trumpeted *Cahiers du Cinéma* symptomatic reading of Ford's film *Young Mr Lincoln* (Editors of *Cahiers du Cinéma*, 1972).

The question then arises, as it does also for Althusser: what are the mechanisms of subject formation? In both Althusser and *Screen* theory the answer is to be found in the application of psychoanalytic concepts in general, and in the work of Lacan in particular. For psychoanalysis, in its focus upon 'the extraordinary adventure which from birth to the liquidation of the Oedipal phase transforms a small animal conceived by a man and a woman into a small human child' (Althusser, 1977: 189), is no more (or less) than the science that studies the basic formation of human subjects. And although so much of the focus of psychoanalytic theory is upon the earliest stages of that formation (Lacan's 'mirror stage'; the Oedipal phase; etc.) the concepts which are developed in this context give access to the later operations of the unconscious and to later processes of subject constitution. It is this which gives rise to the emerging strategy, already seen with Metz, of applying Lacan's ideas metaphorically to the circumstances of film spectatorship. I shall pick up that thread later, in Chapter 6. For the present, however, we must give a little more thought to the role of psychoanalytic concepts in the further development of *Screen* theory.

This is not easy. Lacan is famously difficult to understand, let alone to summarize, and while it is one thing to recognize a *prima facie* case for psychoanalytic concepts in examining subject formation, it is quite another to grasp the full detail of their application when faced with the style in which Lacan typically presents his ideas. Consider, for example, the following superficially simple passage from his well-known essay 'The Signification of the Phallus':

> For the phallus is a signifier, a signifier whose function, in the intra-subjective economy of the analysis, lifts the veil perhaps from the function it performed in the mysteries. For it is the signifier intended to designate as a whole the effects of the signified, in that the signifier conditions them by its presence as a signifier. (Lacan, 1977: 285)

These two sentences defy clear understanding, and while the first, though highly condensed, may reasonably be argued to depend on already grasping the whole framework of Lacan's thinking, the second is problematic simply because of the twists and imprecisions of its construction. As it happens, I believe I know to what it alludes. But it is precisely that allusive character of Lacanian writing which makes it so difficult to grasp with any certainty. And lest any reader think that I am perpetrating a deception by removing the passage from the context in which it appears, I insist that nowhere in that essay is there a contextualization which will ease this problem of interpretation.

Although I am not positively disposed to such wilfully obscure writing, my observation here is not intended as a specific criticism of Lacan nor of those theories which utilize his work. I am concerned, rather, to underline the difficulty of dealing with Lacanian psychoanalytic concepts, and to suggest how strong is the potential for ambiguity, misunderstanding and disagreement in the application of such ideas in cultural studies. Thus, although there are clear and useful accounts of the role of Lacanian concepts in *Screen* theory – Lapsley and Westlake (1988) comes to mind – I doubt that any summary would command widespread agreement among those who were party to these developments. Here, therefore, I shall only be concerned with some of the foundational ideas as they were mediated into cultural studies via *Screen* theory, and even then only in the most schematic and restricted form. This will be sufficient to the task in hand, that of characterizing the basic elements of *Screen* theory.

Lacan reconstructs Freudian theory in terms of the insights afforded by structural linguistics and by structuralism more generally. There are many points at which one might begin an exposition, but since we have already had a passing encounter with it in the context of Metz' semiotics, the 'mirror stage' will serve that purpose here. The account of the mirror stage grew, for Lacan, from 'the startling spectacle of the infant in front of the mirror' (Lacan, 1977: 1). The infant (prior to the age of 18 months) encounters and responds enthusiastically to its image in the mirror. It sees itself, misrecognizes *self* as an ideal ego, as a whole, in the image. Lacan (*ibid*: 2) puts it thus: 'This jubilant assumption of his specular image by the child at the *infans* stage, still sunk in his motor incapacity and nursling dependence, would seem to exhibit in an exemplary situation the symbolic matrix in which the *I* is precipitated in a primordial form, before it is objectified in the dialectic of identification with the other, and before language restores to it, in the universal, its function as subject.'

This passage leads out to many of the key features of Lacan's thinking which played a part in *Screen* theory. In the mirror phase, 'the *I*,' Lacan says, 'is precipitated in primordial form'. In effect, the infant's encounter with the mirror image is the first step along the road toward the constitution of a subject, a self. It is a pre-linguistic and pre-symbolic step, taken in the subjective domain that Lacan speaks of as the Imaginary, but it is also a misrecognition (Lacan's term *méconnaissance* carries additional meanings relating to misknowing) of the 'Ideal-I' as unified. Later, in the infant's encounter with language and, more generally, with what Lacan calls the Symbolic, the process of subject constitution is continued. This is customarily formulated in relation to the *fort-da* game. Freud observed his grandson throwing away and recovering a cotton-reel, accompanied by the repeated cries of '*fort*' (off it goes) and '*da*' (here it is), a game he interpreted primarily as an attempt by the infant to deal with the absence of the mother but also as a beginning process in the construction of a symbolic universe. Lacan extends this such that *fort* and *da* become signifiers of presence/absence, foundations, as it were, of the difference system of language. Then, later still, in the Oedipal phase, the infant encounters the full force of the Symbolic, subjected through language to the 'Name-of-the-Father', to the Law, made into a nascent social subject via the mechanism of the castration complex.

Of course, the apparent phasing of this description should not be taken literally. What is captured here, rather, is the sense of subject formation being intimately connected with the acquisition and character of language. 'The castration complex is seen to complete, in its establishment of differences, the process inaugurated by the mirror phase and the Fort/Da game in which subjectivity is organised by the same structures as language' (Coward and Ellis, 1977: 115). The slogan with which Lacan's work is so often characterized is 'the unconscious is structured like a language', a phrase which, as always with Lacan, may be open to many readings but which certainly suggests the centrality of difference relations in the constitution of subjectivity as much as in the constitution of language. To become a subject is to find a place in a system of representations, to be constituted through the Symbolic as a seemingly unified self.

Now this is more or less the claim that Althusser borrows in constructing his view of interpellation. But even on this deliberately thin account of Lacanian theory it is not clear that subject formation and interpellation are ideal bedfellows. Interpellation has a certain mechanistic quality, a sense of constraint and fixity. Indeed, that was its attraction to those eager to explore the ideological role of film. In the way in which it was adopted by *Screen* theory it offered texts as capturing readers within ideology by virtue of constituting them as subjects. Later *Screen* theory, however, sought to build more on the processual aspects of Lacanian thinking than on the restrictive, text-determinist framework derived from Althusser, and it is certainly true that there are aspects of Lacan's theory which can be used to examine the constant play of signification in subject constitution. Arguably it is this inflection of psychoanalytic theory which has become increasingly prominent in more recent work on film spectatorship. Although that development is beyond the scope of the present discussion (for a good account see Mayne, 1993) I shall return to it in Chapter 6. There I shall examine the remarkable alliance between subject-positioning theory and feminism which was first developed from within *Screen* theory in Mulvey's seminal paper 'Visual Pleasure and Narrative Cinema' (1975).

Texts, subjects, theories

Mulvey's essay appeared in *Screen* in autumn 1975 at a crucial point in the journal's intellectual history. The very next issue was to see a statement from four Editorial Board members taking issue with the journal's burgeoning use of psychoanalytic concepts (Buscombe *et al.*, 1975/76) and two issues after that the same four resigned from the Board. Among the reasons that they gave were the obscurity and inaccessibility of writing in *Screen* and its 'unsound and unproductive' political-cultural analysis (Buscombe *et al.*, 1976). One issue later and the journal's associate editors had gone, either voluntarily or by excision, leaving the field to *Screen* theory's true believers. I mention these ancient dramas not to make a point about the substance of what was at issue (though as an excised associate editor I felt then, as I do now, that the dissenters' position had some force to it) but to underline how powerful were the intellectual disagreements of the time and how all encompassing the theoretical commitments. Whether for or against, participants in these disputes saw themselves as part of the key cultural and political developments of the period. The issues that concerned them may seem arcane now, but in the mid-1970s they appeared vital to the further growth of film theory and to cultural studies more generally.

So, indeed, it was to prove, in as much as *Screen* theory not only originated the powerful 'subject-positioning' tradition in cultural studies, with its reliance on the apparatus of Lacanian psychoanalysis, but also provided the terms in opposition to which a range of subsequent approaches to cultural analysis were formed. Yet it is still difficult to characterize *Screen* theory as a consistent whole. Short textbook summaries, such as that in Turner (1990: 106–109), rightly focus upon the centrality of textual construction of subjectivity to the theory, offering an account of culture in which texts ideologically constrain their 'readers' by restricting the subject positions that they can occupy. But that is at best a tendency in *Screen* theory, rather than an always completed achievement, and right through the 1970s these ideas were worked at and amended both within and beyond the pages of the journal. So, for example, when John Ellis came to write the Introduction to the first collection of readings from *Screen* (published in 1977) he made much of the lack of final closure in the kind of textual analysis found in *S/Z* and the *Cahiers du Cinéma* account of *Young Mr Lincoln*. 'The conception of the productivity of the text,' he wrote, 'throws into doubt whether there are any films which "unproblematically reproduce dominant ideologies": the work of production is always a matter of establishing positions rather than reproducing them.' This, he suggested, had led some writers to think in terms of 'the constant repositioning of a (non-unitary, radically heterogeneous) subject' (Ellis, 1977: n.p.). Whatever else it may be, this is hardly the language to be expected from a simple model of ideological constraint through subject positioning. It is, rather, the product of a constantly developing body of thought which at any given moment was composed of elements that did not necessarily sit entirely easily with each other.

In this context, then, there is no doubt that the proponents of *Screen* theory were fully aware that there were complex interactive processes involved in the relations between 'readers', 'texts' and ideology; to suggest otherwise (as some accounts have) is to perpetrate something of a calumny upon the journal's work. Even so, the theoretical and methodological choices that were made in constructing *Screen* theory inevitably had consequences for quite how those processes were to be understood and, therefore, set limits upon the ways in which the relationship between texts and readers could be conceptualized. Let us examine some of those limits by drawing together *Screen* theory's concept of ideology, its emphasis on psychoanalytic theory, its understanding of the subject, and its conception of reader–text relations. Though this may be a somewhat artificial synthesis, a convenient fabrication that never quite existed in this form, it will serve to suggest the broad thrust of *Screen* theory's ontological and theoretical commitments.

We must begin with ideology, which was a key concept in British cultural studies generally in the 1970s, so much so that one retrospective observer (Carey, 1989: 97) noted that 'British cultural studies could be described just as easily and perhaps more accurately as ideological studies for they assimilate, in a variety of complex ways, culture to ideology'. At its least elaborated, this meant that a loose concept of ideology was widely seen as a useful way to frame cultural analysis, both socially and politically. If forms of culture could be shown to be 'ideological', to serve particular social interests, then that would lead to identification of specific social consequences and, therefore, provide a basis for critical political analysis. In *Screen* theory however, as we have seen, the preferred theory of ideology was derived from Althusser's 'ideology-in-general', a version of the concept which set aside the 'sectional interests' aspect of the loose usage (for Althusser that was a matter for the analysis of ideolo*gies*) in favour of a highly generalized account of the unavoidable construction of subjects within ideology. In this view, people were 'interpellated' by systems of discourse, constituted as subjects by the cultural materials that they encountered, 'always-already' positioned by the ideologies in which they found themselves caught.

In its original form this account conceived social agents as, more or less, victims of ideology, and as it was applied in *Screen* theory it led toward an analysis of reader–text relations which was profoundly text-driven. Films, like cultural texts more generally, were seen to constrain readers, to provide an inscribed subject position ensuring that the text was understood in specific ways. In such a model it is difficult to conceptualize independence or resistance on the part of readers; there appears little room for negotiation or ambiguity. As Turner (1990: 107) concisely puts it: 'in *Screen* theory, texts always and irresistibly tell us how to understand them', and even the rather more positively disposed Lapsley and Westlake (1988: 52) observe that in the Althusserian phase of *Screen* theory 'the central emphasis throughout was on the text's power to determine the subject's response'. The degree to which this tendency is ameliorated by the turn toward psychoanalytic concepts is neither clear nor agreed. Lapsley and Westlake follow up their above observation by invoking Heath's Lacanian-influenced later concern with 'a dialectic of the subject' in which, as they summarize it, 'meaning and subjectivity come into being together, each engendering the other in a process of endless dialectic' (*ibid*: 53). This they believe to be part of a significant move away from the restrictions of the Althusserian view of ideology and subject constitution. Others less friendly to the *Screen* project – for example those working within the Centre for Contemporary Cultural Studies during the 1970s, such as Hall (1980c) and Morley (1980a) – are not convinced that psychoanalytic concepts are adequate to this task. For them, the psychoanalytically based account of the constitution of the subject is insufficient to comprehend 'particular discourses or historically specific ideologies in definite social formations' (Hall, 1980c: 161). Unable to handle social variation in the operation of ideology and subjectivity, the psychoanalytic framework tends instead to reduce it to supposedly universal processes.

It is this charge of misleading reductionism that is most commonly (and most persuasively) levelled at *Screen* theory's use of the psychoanalytic perspective. It is not hard to see why. Although Lacan's structuralist adaptation of Freudian thought does make radical changes in some areas, it still uses concepts which by their very nature refer to essentially trans-cultural processes. The mirror stage, Oedipal relations, castration anxiety, Name-of-the-Father, the Phallus as signifier, all this familiar apparatus presumes to identify aspects of human subject formation which operate regardless of specific social circumstances. Such universal claims are, of course, fundamental to the psychoanalytic project. Inevitably this gives rise to a marked tension between psychoanalytic theories and those more sociological or historical perspectives within which socio-cultural variation is a defining feature. Sometimes this can be a constructive tension, as it arguably was in the work of the Frankfurt School. But for that to be so, it is first necessary that the concepts derived from each theoretical 'side' are conceived as non-reductive and so open to comparative judgement and, if necessary, mutual modification. In the case of *Screen* theory this would be difficult since in its major formulations it appears to presuppose the absolute primacy of psychoanalytic processes in the constitution of subjectivity. Everything in this conceptual domain is understood in relation to the subject; little or nothing in relation to the diverse social circumstances in which subjectivity is daily deployed, negotiated and reconstructed. In short, within *Screen* theory the category of 'the subject' is reified.

The practical consequences of this reification can be seen in the characteristic ways in which *Screen* theory handles the concepts of text and reader. The (film) text – for all the formal emphasis on 'productivity' in post-structuralism – is still understood as the seat of determinate effects upon individual agents. The sequence is something like this: texts (and discourses) carry ideology; ideology operates primarily through the constitution of subjects; subjects are formed through universal psychoanalytic processes; and individuals are unavoidably on the receiving end of such constitutive mechanisms. What is not theorized or theorizable in these terms is how real social subjects – assuming that such an ontological entity is permitted within the terms of *Screen* theory – relate to the subject positions prescribed for them by texts and discourses. Are they active agents with the freedom to accept, reject or modify the position that they are offered for reading a text? Or does the formation of subjectivity in basic psychoanalytic processes constrain agents in terms of structures that are built into the unconscious? And what of multiple interpellation? Faced with the plurality of subject positions on offer in the diverse discourses of modern society, how do agents grapple with the evident potential for contradiction and inconsistency? And what of textual polysemy? Is it purely dependent upon the terms of subject constitution, or do we need further concepts which will give us access to the social construction of meaning in reader–text relations?

Although I have deliberately framed those questions rhetorically, as we shall see in later chapters they have proved real enough in the subsequent development of cultural studies. *Screen* played a hugely significant part in setting the terms within which such questions could be posed, and, because of the intellectual force with which *Screen* theorists developed their position, they obliged aspiring opponents to grapple with issues which otherwise might not have come to the fore. That is very much to their credit. By the end of the 1970s, however, the journal's period of ascendancy was over, and the focus for the now rapidly growing cultural studies movement shifted elsewhere. But *Screen* theory has left its mark, indirectly in shaping a series of concerns with textuality and subjectivity that others were to take up in different ways, and more directly in initiating the use of psychoanalytic theory in the analysis of culture. In so doing they developed one strand of the kind of 'top-down' thinking which was to prove so important in the formation of cultural studies, in this particular variation emphasizing the power of ideological constraint over social agents as that was channelled through psychoanalytic processes. There is a certain irony here. Post-structuralism is distinctive in its movement away from the more formal and mechanistic applications of the Saussurian *langue/parole* model toward a concept of the 'productivity' of the text. Yet its specific realization in *Screen* theory, where it is mediated through selected aspects of the work of Althusser and Lacan, sees that productivity primarily in relation to the textual constitution of subjects and not in the diverse ways in which agents actually read and use texts.

Finally, and apart from these matters of theoretical substance, *Screen* theory also had a less obvious but nonetheless significant impact on the epistemological presuppositions that informed the growth of cultural studies. This was perhaps the first body of coherent cultural studies thinking to put such a distinctive emphasis on theory and theorizing. Not, it should be noted, 'theory' in the instrumentalist sense of that term where theories are always seen as essentially provisional instruments for understanding the real world, frameworks always open to revision in the light of evidence or competition from other candidate theories. The tacit epistemology of *Screen* theory was much grander than that. It adopted from both Althusser and psychoanalysis a fundamentally conventionalist practice in which theorizing is all-encompassing, a source of terms within which the world is both constituted and understood as a totality. Theory here becomes a kind of belief system which unites evaluation and interpretation into the moment of theorizing. Once the framework is accepted, those features of the phenomenal world which are capable of assimilation are incorporated; those which are not are simply excluded. This use of theory – as a kind of interpretative, philosophical world-view – continues to inform cultural studies to the present day, even if the specific terms employed are no longer those advanced in the pages of *Screen* in the 1970s. It too is part of the *Screen* theory inheritance.

5 *Resisting the Dominant*

In recent years it has become commonplace to suggest that the Birmingham Centre for Contemporary Cultural Studies (henceforth, the CCCS) was the main locus for the flowering of modern cultural studies. As I have already observed in Chapter 1, this claim is misleading. Not because the CCCS was insignificant in the development of cultural studies – clearly it was not – but more because our understanding of the complex interrelations between the various intellectual traditions involved in this history is restricted by such one-sided claims. From the perspective of the present study, the CCCS figures as one among several environments within which the characteristic theories and methods of cultural studies emerge. Accordingly, it is essential to understand the CCCS' distinctive analytic contribution in context: both in relation to other contemporary influences and in relation to the older traditions on which the Centre itself drew. Only then might we hope to make even a provisional judgement on its role in the rise of cultural studies.

But where should one begin when faced with such a complex heritage? Since we have just discussed *Screen* theory in some detail, and since that very term was coined in the 1970s by members of the CCCS as they sought to grapple with *Screen*'s forays into structuralism and psychoanalysis, then a convenient place to embark upon an analytic dissection of the CCCS position is in their response to *Screen* theory. On the face of it, the two approaches had much in common. Both initially rejected the traditional mass culture condemnation of popular forms. Both sought to work with and amend the tenets of historical materialism as they (differently) perceived that mode of analysis. And both saw structuralism as initiating a radical shift in theories of signification, representation, and culture more generally. They parted ways, however, in how they made the move from structuralism to poststructuralism, the CCCS viewing *Screen* theory's growing dependence on Lacanian concepts with considerable scepticism. Hall (1980c) conceptualized this shift in terms of a transition from what he called semiotics 1 to semiotics 2, the latter coming to emphasize above all an attempt to theorize 'the subject' in psychoanalytic terms. Semiotics 1 had focused upon the production of meaning, and in so doing formed one of the major influences on the CCCS as well as on *Screen*. Semiotics 2, however, espoused additional theoretical and methodological positions that the CCCS considered to be fundamentally at odds with its own developing project.

These differences revolved around three interrelated themes, all finally traceable to the CCCS' insistence on maintaining a distinctive explanatory role for the realm of the social. The first and most profound disagreement directly reflected this basic ontological difference between the two schools of thought. *Screen*, the CCCS argument ran, gave ultimate primacy to psychoanalytic processes, with the result, as Hall (1980c: 160) put it, that '[e]xcept in a largely ritual sense, any substantive reference to social formation has been made to disappear'. Yet historical materialism, a theoretical commitment presumed to be common to both approaches, required and proposed an understanding of the specificity of particular social forms at defined historical moments. To the CCCS, therefore, the Lacanian turn in *Screen* theory was entirely incompatible with this requirement of historical materialism. *Screen* theorists, of course, felt otherwise (Coward, 1977; Coward and Ellis, 1977) but fortunately we have no need to arbitrate that dispute here. It is sufficient for present purposes to recognize that the CCCS brought to bear a more direct and active sense of the autonomy of the social world than that typically found in *Screen* theory. This reflected a difference in intellectual inheritance. *Screen* theorists embraced a whole range of influences from modern European thought, incorporating a strong anti-humanist, anti-empiricist and anti-sociological emphasis. In contrast, CCCS thinking drew not only upon the more determinist elements in the so-called 'structuralist' marxism of Louis Althusser, but also upon the positive sense of social agency found both in the 'culture and civilisation' tradition and in the work of Gramsci. Hence their insistence upon the importance of an active social agent rather than a reductive psychoanalytic 'subject'.

Inevitably, then, it was with *Screen*'s development of subject positioning theory that the CCCS critics were most at odds. In *Screen* theory, Hall (1980c: 159) argued, 'attempt[s] to relate ideologies to political and economic practices, to their functioning and effectivity in specific social formations and in specific historical conjunctures, have been translated on to the terrain of "the subject"', an achievement managed via a series of what were, to him, illegitimate reductions. This is seen most clearly in the contrast between the subject-in-general of *Screen* theory, constituted in trans-historical and trans-cultural psychoanalytic processes, and the specific historical subject, constituted through a variety of potentially contradictory discursive interpellations. In developing this aspect of their critique, Morley (1980a) draws on Pêcheux's concept of 'interdiscourse' and Laclau's non-Lacanian account of interpellation, arguing for a notion of contradictory and unstable processes of subject positioning which have to be understood in variable social and historical contexts. *Screen* theory, he suggests (*ibid*: 169), 'constantly elides the concrete individual, his/her constitution as a "subject-for-discourse", and the discursive subject positions constituted by specific discursive practices and operations'. Subjects, it must be recognized, have their own histories and operate in concrete social circumstances.

This concern with multiple positioning leads immediately to the second of the themes that characterize the CCCS response to *Screen* theory: the opposition between textual determinacy and textual polysemy. As we saw in Chapter 4, there is an unresolved tension in later *Screen* theory between the desire to see 'texts' as determining the subject positions from which they can be 'read' – a view powerfully developed in the first phase of subject-positioning theory – and a more typically post-structuralist emphasis on the 'productivity' of reading as that was conceptualized in, for example, Barthes' work after *S/Z*. In the CCCS account, the significance of this tension in *Screen*'s position is played down. *Screen* theory is seen as irreducibly text-driven, with the Lacanian apparatus used to define fundamental unconscious processes of subject constitution which are replayed in reader–text relations. 'But this,' Morley (1980a: 167) argues, 'runs counter to two of the most important advances previously established by structural linguistics: the essentially polysemic nature of signs and sign-based discourses, and the interrogative/expansive nature of all readings'.

Again we have no need to arbitrate this disputed interpretation of *Screen* theory. All that needs noting is that the CCCS position does indeed lean rather more toward viewing reader–text relations in polysemic and interrogative terms than did their *Screen* contemporaries, a position that is hardly unexpected given the CCCS commitment to a concept of active agency. This commitment did not always sit easily with their avowed historical materialism, however, and the Centre expended much intellectual energy in trying to chart a safe marxist passage between the Scylla of textual determinism and the Charybdis of productive reading. This led them toward the concept of 'preferred reading' in an attempt to retain a Gramscian concern with ideological dominance and hegemony. '[A] text of the dominant discourse *does* privilege or prefer a certain reading,' Morley (*ibid*) suggests, immediately after castigating *Screen* theory for losing sight of the polysemic emphases central to structuralism. Although this was to prove a difficult claim to sustain in the context of the CCCS' empirical work, their evident desire to maintain a socially determining concept of ideology was to be formative in much of the Centre's thinking.

This, the third theme, is perhaps best caught in the expression 'struggle in ideology'. For the CCCS the operation of ideology, while real enough in its consequences, is never an automatic process of subject constitution or, indeed, of any other irresistible mechanism. Dominant ideologies can always be confronted; readings always contested. The significance of culture, therefore, is that it is a vital terrain on which the struggle between domination and resistance is fought. *Screen*'s strongly text-driven analysis and their use of Lacanian concepts makes it 'impossible to construct . . . an adequate concept of "struggle" in ideology' (Hall, 1980c: 161). The work of ideology is precisely that; it must be worked at if it is to function, negotiated in a context of potentially contradictory interpellations, polysemic signs and multiple readings. The relation between classes, discursive formations and ideology is far more complex than *Screen*'s concepts can encompass, and much of the CCCS project of the late 1970s and the 1980s seeks to theorize this relation more adequately.

It is to this project that we must now turn – the CCCS attempt to formulate a general approach to cultural analysis from a synthesis of the various intellectual traditions that informed their critical response to *Screen* theory. Again, structuralism is the key precipitating factor, although it is structuralism's association with the CCCS' other crucial influences that is central in forming the terms of their framework. I shall consider the elements that make up their position under three broad headings. First, the relationship they sought to forge between structuralism and certain elements of the 'culture and civilization' tradition. Secondly, their views on ideology, class, hegemony, and associated concepts. Thirdly, their attempt to conceptualize media communication and semiotic polysemy using the encoding/decoding model. In each of these areas Stuart Hall, first Assistant Director and then Director of the Centre and a major influence on it during these crucial years, provides us with key texts. To ease the task of exposition for myself, and of understanding for the reader, I shall use the Hall texts as my main sources. Inevitably this will lead me to neglect some of the rich variation found in the Centre's detailed work. In the cause of achieving a general analytic understanding of the CCCS approach, however, that is unavoidable.

Culturalism and structuralism

It was in his influential and much-quoted essay 'Cultural studies: two paradigms' that Hall (1980b) most clearly sought to conceptualize the relationship between the culturalist and structuralist traditions in the foundations of CCCS thinking. The essence of his argument is that the culturalist tradition (epitomized in the work of Hoggart, Williams and Thompson) occasioned the emergence of cultural studies as a 'distinctive problematic'. But this developing strand of thought was 'interrupted by the arrival on the intellectual scene of the "structuralisms"' (*ibid*: 64) which, while not without problems of their own, focused attention upon, and to some degree compensated for, the failings of the culturalist tradition. Building upon the 'best elements' drawn from both traditions will, Hall suggests, provide a basis for conceptualizing the core issues of cultural studies.

All this, of course, is not inconsistent with the account of the rise of cultural studies given earlier in this book. The devil, however, is in the detail, and when one examines the gloss that Hall puts on both 'structuralism' and 'culturalism' the theoretical specificity of his case becomes more apparent. Let us begin with culturalism. Here he takes Hoggart, Williams and Thompson as each representing a particular kind of break with earlier traditions. Hoggart he sees as re-forming the terms of critical debate as that had been found in Leavis' work and in prevailing concerns about the rise of mass society and mass culture. Williams, while also responding to that same set of critical issues, establishes more of a break with *theoretical* tradition, moving through the 'culture-and-society' analysis of *Culture and Society* and rapidly on to the more significant conceptual innovations found in *The Long Revolution*. Thompson (in *The Making of the English Working Class*) is also seen to make a significant break with earlier forms of thought, but this time with the kinds of economism, determinism and evolutionism that had been characteristic of much orthodox marxist analysis. In Hall's ensuing discussion, it is clear that Hoggart is the least important of these three to his reading of cultural studies; it is on Williams, and to a lesser degree Thompson, that he focuses attention.

This is a significant pointer to the way in which the CCCS was to develop, for, unlike Hoggart, Williams and Thompson were both embroiled (sometimes with each other) in debates central to the emergence of 'new left' thinking. It is this theoretical discussion that Hall considers to be fundamental to the emergence of cultural studies, reminding us that his and the CCCS' preferred terms of the period are marxist in their general tenor, if not in all their detail. He sees Williams, therefore, as a key figure, uniting the recognition that culture is 'threaded through *all* social practices' (Hall, 1980b: 60) with an attempt to reformulate the typical base–superstructure approach to culture found in orthodox marxist analysis. This view Hall characterizes as 'radical interactionism' in which human practices are conceived to stand in complex inter-relation, rather than specific (material) elements being singled out as ultimate determinants. In developing these ideas, Hall claims, Williams may still only be 'skirting the problem of determinancy' (*ibid*) rather than resolving it, but it remains an important topic with which Williams would continue to grapple in his later work. Indeed, it is in response to Thompson's critique of *The Long Revolution*, Hall suggests, that Williams recognizes the significance of the idea of 'struggle' in the cultural domain and the consequent importance of Gramsci's concept of 'hegemony' for rethinking the relation between culture and the other elements of social life. These were ideas that would become central to the whole CCCS project.

How, then, does Hall summarize the culturalist tradition? Standing in opposition to models of the relationship between ideal and material that routinely give primacy to the economic base over the cultural superstructure, culturalism 'conceptualizes culture as interwoven with all social practices; and those practices, in turn, as a common form of human activity: sensuous human praxis, the activity through which men and women make history' (*ibid*: 63). But this is not the whole story. Also central to culturalism is what Hall calls the 'experiential pull' of the perspective, an aspect which, along with its emphasis on the active contribution of social agents to making their own history, is a key element in forming the basic 'humanism' of the position. In Hall's view this leads culturalism into methodological difficulties, not least the tendency to seek to grasp, to *understand* in its totality, the entire experience of social and cultural processes and therefore to resist any form of analytical abstraction that might serve to break down those processes into determinately related elements. Thus, the typical mode of understanding fostered by this (tacit) epistemology – seen, for example, in Williams' 'structures of feeling' – is expressive and experiential, tending to focus upon 'lived experience' at the expense of analytic understanding.

To this developing system of ideas Hall counterposes structuralism or, rather, 'the stucturalisms'. In using the plural he recognizes that the structuralist tradition is rather more varied than the culturalist, and takes to task, therefore, those theorists of the period who, much influenced by Althusser, saw the concept of ideology as integral to structuralism. Significantly, given Hall's and the CCCS' subsequent commitment to a form of cultural analysis in which ideology is a central concept, he stresses the importance of Lévi-Strauss to the structuralist project. He singles out several features of Lévi-Strauss' thought as being of particular significance: his concern with the production of meaning in signifying practices; his emphasis on culture rather than on ideology; and his application of a 'logic of arrangement' to the elements of a system rather than a simple, reductive logic of determinacy. This engagement with Lévi-Strauss enables Hall to read Althusser in particular, and structuralism in general, as offering a rather richer approach to the problem of examining the determinate conditions of social life than was apparent in other Althusser-influenced work of the period. Furthermore, while avoiding the Lacanian turn in *Screen* theory's reading of Althusser, he is nonetheless able to retain a 'structuralist' concept of ideology in which signifying practices are seen to impose upon human agents an 'imaginary' relation to the real.

In this context, then, Hall goes on to consider three positive features of structuralist thought, all notable because they stand in stark contrast to key presuppositions of culturalism. These three virtues, in Hall's account of them, are: first, a renewed emphasis on the importance of conceptualizing determinate conditions in cultural analysis; secondly, a recognition of the inevitability of abstraction in revealing otherwise concealed relationships and structures, thus allowing specific practices to be understood in the context of the larger 'totality'; and lastly, the 'decentering of experience' and consequent theorizing of it as a product of ideology. The significance of these features to Hall and to the CCCS' developing position lies in their potential for 'correcting' perceived limitations in the culturalist paradigm.

First, culturalism can fall all too easily into what Hall describes as 'naïve humanism', overstating the freedom of agency and consciousness and thereby neglecting 'the fact that, in capitalist relations, men and women are placed and positioned in relations which constitute them as agents' (*ibid*: 67). Secondly, culturalism is also prone to resist abstraction, failing to recognize the necessity for a methodology of analysis that permits understanding across and between different levels of abstraction. Without such a method and a concomitant conception of the complex totality of human relations, culturalism is incapable of properly grasping the character of specific social practices in their larger context. Thirdly, although the concept of ideology does feature in the work of the culturalist tradition, their central concern with the category of experience 'imposes a barrier between culturalism and a proper conception of "ideology"' (*ibid*: 69). So, in all three areas, structuralist thought can provide a significant corrective to the inherent limitations of culturalism.

This is not just a straightforward task of synthesis, however, and Hall is careful to suggest that neither paradigm as presently constituted would provide adequate conceptual foundations for cultural studies. For culturalism, too, must contribute to subsequent theorizing, its key strength lying in its emphasis on consciousness, struggle, active intervention and agency. It is in these respects that culturalism can compensate for structuralism's tendency to produce a somewhat mechanistic and over-deterministic model of human activity. Notwithstanding that nod to culturalism, we should recognize quite how far Hall's argument is leaning toward the structuralism side of the structuralism–culturalism dyad. While he views structuralism as compensating for limitations in the culturalist paradigm in several key areas of theory and method, culturalism itself contributes to the 'synthesis' in rather more restricted ways. Although its focus on agency and struggle is undeniably important – it will provide the point of departure for a more thoroughgoing introduction of Gramscian ideas into cultural studies – it is difficult to resist the conclusion that the most significant and innovative elements in CCCS thinking at this time are more deeply influenced by the structuralist than by the culturalist paradigm. But, whatever that balance, it is strikingly clear that the inflection that Hall gives to both structuralism and culturalism is predominantly marxist, even though, as he recognizes, both traditions incorporate substantial non-marxist elements. This finds important expression in the CCCS' attempt to further develop cultural studies via the interrelated concepts of ideology, hegemony and class, and it is to this aspect of their project that we now turn.

Ideology, hegemony, class

In 1977 the Centre devoted their tenth collection of Working Papers in Cultural Studies to the topic of ideology, and these were published a year later in book form as *On Ideology* (CCCS, 1978).

Agreeing that, as Hall (1978: 28) put it, '[i]deology is one of the least developed "regions" in marxist theory', they examined the work of Althusser, Gramsci, Lukács and Poulantszas with a view to developing a more cogent conceptualization of ideology for the purposes of cultural studies. These were hectic years in British 'new left' thought. Althusserianism had swept all before it in the first half of the 1970s, reviving a well established tradition of fierce debate within left politics and promoting much more interest in matters of theory and epistemology. The CCCS, like all groups with a claim to developing a leftist critical analysis of modern society, was caught up in this widespread recovery of marxist theory and in its evident concern with ideology and with 'superstructural' elements more generally.

That said, the CCCS also recognized that none of the competing frameworks offered a ready-made solution to the 'problem of ideology'; hence the need to examine the wide variety of marxist theories then in circulation rather than immediately commit all resources, as some of the 'purer' Althusserians had, to one approach above all others. Of course, given the CCCS' culturalist inheritance it makes sense (in retrospect, at least) that they should be attracted by the more 'active' elements in Gramsci's thought and somewhat resistant to the deterministic aspects of Althusser's 'structuralist' appropriation of it. But they were still significantly influenced by Althusser's account of ideology, while also recognizing that '[t]here is no systematic theory of ideology in the work of Antonio Gramsci' (Hall *et al.*, 1978: 45) and therefore that the task of developing an adequate understanding of the role of ideology in culture would not be easy. Indeed, right through the period of CCCS concern with these issues it is possible to see quite deep conceptual divisions, both among those who were engaged in developing the general theory itself and between these theorists and others within the Centre whose work had a different focus.

Nevertheless, by the early 1980s a broad consensus was emerging on the utility of the Gramscian way of framing a theory of ideology, the principal features of which can be seen in Hall's well-known attempt to formulate these ideas in the cause of a critical approach to media studies (Hall, 1982). I shall use this discussion as an initial focus for my account of CCCS views on the role of ideology in culture and in cultural studies more generally.

Hall's argument – as so often in his work of this period – is directed at our ways of understanding the role of the mass media in modern societies. He locates the orthodox (behavioural and effects) tradition of mass communications research in the context of the rise to dominance in the 1950s of pluralism as *the* social science model of modern industrial society. In this account, there were social and political conflicts, certainly, but all regulated and contained within a framework of broad consensus. The mass media functioned as a channel of influence, both in processes of pluralist decision making and, more generally, as an expression of the overall consensus. As the 1960s progressed, however, doubts of various kinds emerged from within pluralist social science about the nature of the presumed consensus and the terms of its formation, and about the ways in which the media's 'signifying practices' defined rather than simply reproduced or 'reflected' reality. For Hall (others have charted it differently) this growing dissent pointed to a common concern with the 'ideological dimension' of social life which he understood as involving 'the winning of a universal validity and legitimacy for accounts of the world which are partial and particular, and to the grounding of these particular constructions in the taken-for-grantedness of "the real"' (Hall, 1982: 65). What pluralism conceived of as a kind of 'natural' consent, critical frameworks were to analyse as an achievement of ideology.

This signals the emergence of what he calls 'the critical

paradigm in media studies' which is concerned to understand the mechanisms by which ideological processes work, and the relation in which such processes stand to 'other practices within a social formation' (*ibid*). Structuralism provides Hall with a way into the first issue, its emphasis upon signification offering concepts appropriate to grasping the ways in which systems of meaning ('cultural inventories' is one term Hall uses for them) are constructed around specific events and how, through the institutions of the mass media, they are made legitimate over and above other possible constructions. Conflict over such processes is centrally important: '[t]he signification of events is part of what has to be struggled over, for it is the means by which collective social understandings are created – and thus the means by which consent for particular outcomes can be effectively mobilized' (*ibid*: 70). Herein lies the 'politics of signification'. If privileged meanings are sustained by their framing within particular signifying structures, then contesting those meanings and revealing the significatory terms via which they come to be 'taken-for-granted' is a vital political function of any critical media studies.

The difficulty with this structuralist-inspired conception is that its access to the 'deep structures' underlying diverse significatory processes is too formalistic to meet the historical needs of Hall's and the CCCS' commitment to a marxist analysis. Over the years, he argues, the network of presuppositions on which taken-for-grantedness (or 'naturalization') rests would change and develop through 'accretion' and 'sedimentation', and any proper understanding of the workings of ideology would need to conceptualize these processes. In effect, it is necessary to historicize structuralist method, replacing the timeless universalism of Lévi-Straussian myth analysis with a more historical conception. It is to Gramsci that Hall turns for appropriate terms, invoking his concept of 'common sense': 'the inventory of traditional ideas, the forms of episodic thinking which provide us with the taken-for-granted elements of our practical knowledge' (*ibid*: 73). Always undergoing adaptation, this 'reservoir of themes and premises' was bound into the very fabric of the social formation.

It is also from Gramsci (and Vološinov) that Hall draws inspiration in extending the idea of the politics of signification in terms of the 'class struggle in language' or, as he expresses it more generally, the 'struggle over meaning'. The generalization is important, of course, since it partially disconnects the idea of contesting ideological meanings from a strictly class location: 'though discourses could become an arena of social struggle, and all discourses entailed certain definite premises about the world, this was not the same thing as ascribing ideologies to classes in a fixed, necessary or determinate way' (*ibid*: 80). Ideology and ideological struggle, therefore, could not be understood as merely reflecting the terms of, say, the economic base; they had 'relative autonomy'. This is not to lose sight of the crucial concept of dominance, however, where a framework may be imposed (by force or 'ideological compulsion') on a subordinate group, but this too must be enlarged in terms of Gramsci's concept of hegemony. Hegemony depends on cultural leadership to control the 'form and level of culture and civilization' in such a way as to sustain the dominant 'social and productive system'. Thus, 'hegemony is understood as accomplished, not without the due measure of legal and legitimate compulsion, but principally by means of winning the active consent of those classes and groups who were subordinated within it' (*ibid*: 85). It is, then, the 'production of consent' that is the key role of the media within a given social formation.

This process of loosening the links between ideology (and, therefore, culture) and class is part of an ongoing shift away from marxist orthodoxy in both Hall's work and that of the CCCS. Compare this 1982 formulation of class, ideology and hegemony, for example, with that found in one of the best-known CCCS products of the mid-1970s: *Resistance through Rituals* (Hall and Jefferson, 1976). The lengthy theoretical overview which begins that volume (Clarke *et al.*, 1976) is in no doubt about the centrality of class to its project. 'In modern societies, the most fundamental groups are the social classes, and the major cultural configurations will be, in a fundamental though often mediated way, "class cultures"' (Clarke *et al.*, 1976: 13). As is well known, they go on to conceptualize working-class youth subcultures in terms of dominance and subordination, examining their double articulation in relation to both the parent working-class culture and the 'hegemonic' dominant culture. Ideology is drawn into the picture in terms that owe a good deal to Althusser, in as much as subcultures are seen to 'solve' problems of material relations in an 'imaginary' way. This view is supported by the familiar passage from Althusser's *For Marx*: 'in ideology men do indeed express, not the real relation between them and their conditions of existence, but *the way* they live the relation between them and the conditions of their existence' (quoted in Clarke *et al.*, 1976: 48).

Gramsci, too, is introduced in familiar terms. 'Hegemony works through ideology, but it does not consist of false ideas, perceptions, definitions. It works *primarily* by inserting the subordinate class into the key institutions and structures which support the power and social authority of the dominant order. It is, above all, in these structures and relations that a subordinate class *lives its subordination*' (*ibid*: 39). Note the emphasis on class here. Hegemonic domination requires consent, secured in civil society through class leadership, a process exemplified in 1950s Britain where it was 'the role of "affluence", as an ideology, to dismantle working-class resistance and deliver the "spontaneous consent" of the class to the authority of the dominant classes' (*ibid*: 40). On this cultural terrain there is resistance, negotiation and struggle as well as dominance, for 'contrary cultural definitions are *always* in play' (*ibid*: 43) where classes seek to 'win space'.

In this discussion class is clearly the central focus, whether in formulating the precise terms in which working-class subcultures relate to parent and dominant cultures, or in defining the general forms within which ideology operates ('imaginary' relations to 'real' conditions) and hegemony is secured. Compared to Hall's later formulations (where 'relative autonomy' of the ideological level is more prominent and groups other than classes feature significantly) the *Resistance through Rituals* position is heavily class oriented. But as CCCS work diversified in the late 1970s and the 1980s class became less central to their analysis, on both theoretical and empirical grounds. Apart from the obvious difficulties experienced by orthodox marxism in incorporating gender and race as significant forms of social differentiation and exploitation, the very concern of the CCCS with the 'struggle in ideology' required a growing recognition that the social groupings around which such struggles coalesced were not always easily reducible to class terms. Hall, in his increasingly Gramscian formulations of the relation between ideology and the material world, had always been careful to use the expression 'classes *and* social groups', allowing that there were significant social groups that required non-class concepts for their proper understanding. By 1983, while still resisting the move of some marxist theorists of ideology toward a model in which endless variation in discourses replaced a class-determined account, the picture he offers is one in which a more general play of social forces is realised in struggle. As an example of the changing position, this passage is worth quoting at length:

Ideas only become effective if they do, in the end, *connect* with a particular constellation of social forces. In that sense, ideological struggle is part of the general social struggle for mastery and

> leadership – in short for hegemony. But 'hegemony' in Gramsci's sense requires, not the simple escalation of a whole class to power, with its fully formed 'philosophy', but the *process* by which a historical bloc of social forces is constructed and the ascendancy of that bloc secured. So the way we conceptualize the relationship between 'ruling ideas' and 'ruling classes' is best thought in terms of the processes of 'hegemonic domination'. (Hall, 1996: 43–44)

As the 1980s progressed, and Hall sought to grapple with the challenge posed to marxist analysis by 'Thatcherism', this shift would become increasingly apparent. Indeed, Sparks (1996b: 97) argues that 'in the current associated with Stuart Hall, the link between marxism and cultural studies was much more contingent and transitory than it once appeared even to its main actors', going on to suggest that its 'productive life' was no more than five to ten years. While that may be slightly less than charitable, clearly Sparks (*ibid*: 98) is correct to suggest that the development of cultural studies involved 'a continual loosening of some of the categories thought to be characteristic of marxism'. Where that leads can conveniently be seen in the main contours of what came to be known as the 'encoding/decoding' model.

Encoding, decoding and polysemy

The encoding/decoding model neatly captures the particular combination of semiotics and hegemony theory around which so much of the CCCS analysis of the media revolved. As we saw at the beginning of this chapter, CCCS thinking was resistant to the textual determinism of early *Screen* theory, arguing instead that the inherent polysemy of significatory practices confounded such a strongly text-driven view and, therefore, that 'audiences' should be understood to be composed of active social agents rather than psychoanalytically formed subjects. In developing a model of communication processes based on the semiotically derived proposition that there were different encoding and decoding 'moments' involved in communication, Hall (1980d, 1997) set the terms for an alternative account of 'reader–text' relations which would be more consistent with the CCCS focus on the 'struggle in ideology'. Furthermore, in seeking to apply this model to a specific case (the *Nationwide* television programme) the CCCS media group were obliged to confront empirical and theoretical problems that would finally lead away from CCCS orthodoxy and toward rather different forms of cultural analysis (Brunsdon and Morley, 1978; Morley 1980b, 1981, 1986, 1992). The later stages of that will concern us rather more in Chapter 7. For the present, the significance of the encoding/decoding model lies in what it can tell us about the mainstream CCCS framework.

The essence of the model is familiar enough, deriving from the basic structuralist insight, if insight it is, that 'meaningful discourse' is always coded. Broadcasting organizations are in the business of producing such encoded messages, based on the 'meaning structures' available to them and located within the frameworks of knowledge, relations of production and technical infrastructure characteristic of such organizations. This is one 'moment' of the communication process. Once constituted in this way the television programme (let us say) is made available to an audience for decoding. They, too, utilize the 'meaning structures' available to them and work within their specific frameworks of knowledge, relations of production and technical infrastructure. This decoding 'moment' yields up the meaning of the discourse. Or, rather, it yields up *a* meaning, in as much as the 'codes of encoding and decoding may not be perfectly symmetrical' (Hall, 1980d: 131) and so the meanings derived by audiences may not coincide with those encoded by broadcasters.

Of course, Hall recognizes that semiotic frameworks of this kind had already changed the ways in which analysts viewed mass media 'content' – structuralist-inspired work on 'texts' was ample testimony to that. In line with CCCS commitment to active agency and ideological contest, however, he is more concerned with the likely impact on our understanding of audiences, and the ways in which they read and respond to media messages. Making use of the analytic distinction between denotative and connotative meanings (by then well known from Barthes' application of it in his early semiology and in *Mythologies*) he relates ideology to the naturalized codes through which connotative meanings are established: 'it is at the connotative *level* of the sign that situational ideologies alter and transform signification'. The sign, already coded at the denotative level, interacts with the broader codes of a culture to 'take on additional, more active, ideological dimensions' (*ibid*: 133). This, of course, opens up potential for polysemy in that given signs may play different connotative roles. But this is not, Hall (*ibid*: 134) argues, a recipe for unrestrained significatory pluralism: '[c]onnotative codes are *not* equal among themselves. Any society/culture tends, with varying degrees of closure, to impose its classifications of the social and political and cultural world. These constitute a *dominant cultural order*.' We decode in terms of the 'mappings' that are available to us, and these mappings constitute the basis for ascribing 'dominant or preferred meanings'. Indeed, 'possible meanings will be organised within a scale which runs from *dominant* to *subordinate*' (Hall, 1997: 30).

In this way the structuralist concept of coding is yoked to an account of culture and ideology in which there are 'structures in dominance' and within which the 'struggle in ideology' is continued. Limits are set on the polysemic implications of structuralist theories by postulating a social world in which there are dominant ideologies through which hegemonic control is sought. But securing hegemony is not automatic; there is always the potential and the actuality of resistance. To get some leverage on this aspect of communication, and to avoid sinking into yet another form of pluralism in which audiences are free to read 'texts' however they wish, Hall offers three 'hypothetical positions' from which audiences may set about their decoding activities. The first he describes as the 'dominant-hegemonic' position, where the television viewer decodes the message 'in terms of the reference code in which it has been encoded' (Hall, 1980d: 136) thus arriving at the 'preferred reading'. Note that there is an assumption here that the initial coding – often mediated through a special sub-code characteristic of broadcasters which he calls the 'professional code' – is cast in terms of the dominant ideology, although the semiotic logic of the process (as opposed to the ontological assumption of ideological dominance) permits coding 'freedom' at either end of the communications chain. The second position is that of the 'negotiated code'. Here decoding involves a mixture of possibilities at different levels: '[i]t accords the privileged position to the dominant definitions of events while reserving the right to make a more negotiated application to "local conditions"' (*ibid*: 137). Inevitably this form of decoding has the potential to give rise to all sorts of contradictions and ambiguities, constituting precisely the kinds of circumstances that broadcasters tend to identify as communication failures. Lastly, the message may be decoded in a way contrary to the dominant coding, understood, that is, from within an alternative reference framework. This is the case of the 'oppositional code', and its use signals fully the presence of the 'struggle in discourse'.

Essentially, then, Hall is here trying to tread a fine line between a position in which consent to relations of dominance and subordination is achieved via media constraint and one which recognizes the complexity and relative 'freedom' of audience reading practices. Compared to earlier 'media manipulation' theories, of whatever political persuasion, the encoding/decoding model does indeed free the audience from the absolute bonds of media determinism. But in the context of the late 1970s post-structuralist concern with 'the free play of signifiers', this division into encoding and decoding moments, and the associated postulation of 'hypothetical decoding positions', smacks of an attempt to impose too restrictive an order on what were increasingly being recognized as more open processes of meaning construction. All decoding is negotiated, surely, but in relation to the text as a complex significatory system, not just a hypothetical 'preferred meaning'. It is significant, therefore, that when CCCS researchers came to make use of the model in their study of *Nationwide*, both in mounting a semiotic analysis of the 'text' and in examining the social determination of meaning among the *Nationwide* audience, they encountered considerable difficulties.

Thus, in the 'critical postscript' to his study of the *Nationwide* audience, Morley (1981) finds it necessary to examine what he considers to be the major problems of the encoding/decoding model. He suggests that there are three main issues: one revolving around the presumed intentionality of the encoder; a second arising because the model tended to see 'television as a conveyor-belt for a pre-given message or "meaning" rather than [seeking] an understanding of the production of meaning in and through practices of signification' (Morley, 1992: 120); and a third relating to the conflation of a variety of reading processes under the one concept of decoding. What lies behind all three, of course, is the fact that, like *Screen* theory, the CCCS position is at heart committed to a 'top-down' view. Although they may not adopt a strong text-determinist line of argument, they nonetheless lay claim to a 'preferred reading' inscribed *within the text* and offer a classification of reading responses (dominant, negotiated and oppositional) which takes that preferred reading as its key reference point. Wren-Lewis (1983: 184) suggests that '[t]his is effectively to reproduce the *Screen* position' and, while that may somewhat overstate the case, his subsequent point is well made that this approach precludes understanding the subject's role in *constituting* signification. Signification requires involvement of the reading agent to complete the process of meaning construction, an activity which cannot properly be understood via a model that sees the message as contained within the text prior to reading. As Wren-Lewis (*ibid*) goes on to observe: '[t]he fact that many decoders will come up with the same reading does not make that meaning an essential part of the text. The power of the text's signifiers to determine a specific set of readings will be constituted by historical subjects, whose place in society/history will enable them to form the same associations and differences, the same signifying patterns.'

So, while postulating a 'preferred reading' does not exactly replicate the terms of subject-positioning theory, the encoding/decoding model does ask that concept to carry a great deal of weight. Morley (1992: 121) observes that its purpose was to link the general case about hegemony to specific processes of communication, a task somewhat confounded by the fact that 'hegemony has on the whole been treated as an abstract concept – referring rather widely to the whole field of cultural process through which "dominant meanings" are constructed – without these particular processes being examined in any detail'. In consequence, the model only coheres by suggesting that broadcasters' products (as a direct result of their 'professional code' and, indirectly, the dominant-hegemonic code) incorporate a preferred reading; that the text itself can be semiotically understood as carrying this pre-determined (by the dominant ideology) meaning; and that the 'reader' accepts, negotiates with, or rejects it. Without the 'preferred reading' to connect the elements, the model would be no more (or less) than a reassertion of the codedness of communication, in which, as I have already observed, all decoding is 'negotiated' but in relation to the whole significatory system and not just a hypothetical dominant meaning. Unfortunately, however, to shelter so much of the process under the 'preferred reading' umbrella serves to conceal rather than expose two vital ingredients of any semiotically sensitive view of readership: the constitutive role played by agents in ascribing meaning to cultural artefacts and the ubiquity of polysemy in complex communications.

Morley (*ibid*: 87) puts the requirement for a 'preferred reading' concept in a rather more qualified way:

> If a notion such as a 'preferred reading' is to have any value, it is not as a means of abstracted 'fixing' of one interpretation over and above others, but as a means of accounting for how, under certain conditions, in particular contexts, a text will be read in a particular way by (at least some sections of) the audience.

But in that case, it will be the general theoretical terms through which conditions, contexts and reading processes are understood that will be the key focus, none of which – either in the *Nationwide* study or elsewhere – are well served by a model in which 'preferred reading' plays a central role. That it came to do so in this particular strand of CCCS thinking is a clear indication of the constraints placed on their work by the dominant ideology/hegemony model with which they chose to realise the project of a critical marxist cultural studies.

Critical cultural studies

This chapter has concentrated on those features of the CCCS project that sought to develop a general account of the role of culture in social life, its embodiment in signifying practices, and its ideo-logical function in securing hegemonic domination. Of course, the Centre produced much more work than that, some of it applying these general theoretical terms in specific areas, some striking out in different directions. Thus, the Race and Politics Group produced a critical examination of racism in Britain which, although con-cerned with both ideology and marxism, did not find ready-made theoretical resources in prevailing CCCS ideas: '[i]t was the frus-trating search for an inter-disciplinary, historical approach which was geared to the contemporary struggle against racism which forced us to turn our own hands to analysis' (CCCS, 1982: 7). Similarly, the Women's Studies Group found itself in some tension with other areas of the Centre's work, in consequence developing its own critical response in which, among other things, it sought 'to avoid a general tendency in CCCS towards an *un*self-conscious use of theoretical language which is one element in perpetuating knowledge as the property of the few' (CCCS Women's Studies Group, 1978: 8). That response formed part of a wider feminist input into cultural studies which will be pursued in more detail in Chapter 6.

As well as these growing general concerns with forms of domi-nation and subordination other than class, the Centre also produced a striking range of empirical work. They documented diverse features of working-class culture (Clarke *et al.*, 1979), engaged with the move toward more ethnographically oriented methods that had become so prominent in 1970s sociology (Hall *et al.*, 1980: Part Two), and provided a foundation for well known and well regarded individual studies such as those by Willis (1977) and Hebdige (1979). As these diverse examples indicate, CCCS projects were hardly homogeneous even during the Centre's heyday. Nevertheless, the position captured in the theoretical 'snapshot' of this chapter does represent the high point of the

Centre's influence on cultural studies, while critical responses to it – from both within and beyond the Centre itself – were instrumental in forming the terms within which cultural studies would develop during the 1980s.

Where, then, did this position face difficulties such that the next wave of cultural studies scholars found it necessary to move on to other issues and utilize different concepts? It is convenient to consider this question under three summarizing headings: class, ideology, and signification. On class, the Centre itself was aware by the 1980s that it had over-emphasized the centrality of class and class cultural formations. This was seen to have led to a relative neglect of other important systems of domination and subjection, notably gender and race, analysis of which was quite properly thought to be essential to any critical cultural studies. Furthermore, in the broader theoretical arena of modern marxism, widespread interest in the role of 'superstructural' elements in sustaining capitalist societies had inevitably reduced the direct significance of class concepts, feeding, as it did, into a more generalized interest in 'ideology' which was itself becoming increasingly disconnected from a simple class base.

In this context, let me again quote Carey's (1989: 97) remark that 'British cultural studies could be described just as easily and perhaps more accurately as ideological studies'. Although posed in general terms, this claim is particularly apposite to the CCCS position, where a focus on ideology informed almost every aspect of their analysis and where culturally mediated relations of dominance and subordination were, therefore, the key relations to be understood. It might be argued, of course, that this gave rise to an approach to cultural studies that systematically neglected those aspects of culture and cultural activity which were not immediately intelligible in terms of dominant and subordinate relations. Certainly, the CCCS view was one that largely *presupposed* the effectiveness of a dominant ideology, despite their evident concern with human agency and the 'struggle in discourse'. In this respect, it must be said, they reflected the widespread commitment to dominant ideology arguments in the marxist theorizing of the period. Yet, as Abercrombie *et al.* (1980) forcefully argue, while still seeking to retain a broad historical materialist position, this presumption is theoretically problematic and empirically inadequate.

Some of the consequences of presupposing a dominant ideology will have been apparent in this chapter's discussion of the CCCS attempt to focus semiotic accounts of signification through the lens provided by hegemony theory. We saw how that framework necessitated a concept of 'preferred' or 'dominant' reading if the conjunction of structuralist analysis of signification and Gramscian marxism was to be maintained. We also saw how the concept of 'preferred reading' restricted the capacity of analyses cast in its terms to grapple with the conjoint issues of polysemy and the constitutive role played by social agents in the construction of meaning. This does not mean, of course, that questions about ideology and domination are unimportant or inappropriate. It suggests, rather, that what Abercrombie (1990) calls 'textual ideology' (that encoded in the text), 'ideology setting' (the processes whereby a text is encoded with ideology) and the 'ideological effect' (on audiences, securing domination) are connected only contingently. '[I]ncoherence, diversity and pluralization characterize all three moments of the ideological process, making each difficult to secure. This makes the proper articulation of textual ideology, ideology setting and ideological effect, necessary for popular culture to be in any sense ideological, even more difficult to secure. There is no principle that organizes the three moments' (*ibid*: 222).

In the 1980s difficulties such as these led cultural studies away from the concept of (dominant) ideology and toward new ways of thinking through the balance between textual (or ideological or cultural) determination, on the one hand, and the constitutive role of human agency in 'reading' texts and constructing meaning, on the other. Various possibilities have emerged, ranging from empirically detailed 'ethnographies' of audiences and their reading practices, through more general attempts to reconceptualize ideas of 'audience' and 'reading', and on to so-called postmodern celebrations of the plurality of the popular. These developments (and their roots in reactions against both *Screen* theory and the CCCS) will be considered further in Chapter 7. But it should be noted here that in the course of these changes one or two worthwhile babies may have been cast out with the bathwater of ideology theory. For the CCCS also bequeathed cultural studies some positive features, most notably their concern to sustain a critical cultural studies, their determination not only to theorize but to treat the consequent theories as requiring empirical demonstration, and putting the problem of determinacy and agency so firmly on the cultural studies agenda. Whatever limitations we may now see in their particular attempt to understand the role of culture in modern societies, those issues do remain central to theory and method in cultural studies.

6 *Gendered Subjects, Women's Texts*

Few would deny the importance of feminism in the development of modern cultural studies. The emergence of so-called Second Wave feminism coincided with the growth of a distinctive body of post-structuralist cultural studies theory, and both women's studies and cultural studies – as Franklin *et al.* (1991: 1) observe in their introduction to the tenth anniversary successor to the CCCS volume *Women Take Issue* – 'have in common a strong link to radical politics outside the academy' as well as a powerful impetus toward an inter-disciplinary focus upon culture, power and oppression. But the relationship is not straightforward. Both traditions have tangled histories of their own, histories which are driven by characteristically different political and analytic concerns as well as being variously and contingently intertwined.

Unsurprisingly, therefore, it is not easy to unpick (or even identify) the knots that have bound feminism and cultural studies together. Those who have sought to do so have often found the task to be one of charting differences as much as overlaps, autonomous developments as much as reciprocal influences.

Students to whom I offer the seminar topic 'Examine the influence of feminism on cultural studies' embrace it enthusiastically only to report ruefully that the references which I provide leave them more confused than enlightened. This is not really the fault of the literature; the question is a very difficult one to address once you try to move beyond a simple pointing up of particular studies or specific innovations. Part of the difficulty stems from the fact that, as Franklin *et al.* (1991: 11) conclude later in their introductory discussion, 'there remain substantial difficulties in defining what might be meant by specifically feminist understandings of culture'. It is this limitation that leads them to restrict the analytic organization of their account, and their volume of readings, to three loose and temporally specific areas of potential overlap between feminism and cultural studies.

Other summarizing projects face similar difficulties, often taking up the challenge by conceiving of a range of 'feminisms' rather than presupposing a single homogeneous feminist framework. Lovell (1995) for example, recognizing the diversity of both cultural studies and feminism, invokes several feminist approaches (among others: cultural feminism, feminist populism, postmodern feminism, black feminism) in the course of introducing her collection of essays on 'feminist cultural studies'. As the sheer range of her two volumes amply illustrates, the mapping task is indeed a formidable one, the variety of work startling in its vigour and diversity. Or, less extensively as befits a more textbook-oriented approach, Storey (1993: 125–126) introduces his account of feminism in cultural studies in terms of the familiar quartet of radical feminism, liberal feminism, Marxist feminism and dual-systems theory. He notes, however, that alternative classifications might also cast some light into the conceptual gloom. And while it is true that such headings as these can provide useful ordering foundations on which to build a systematic account of the interaction of feminism and cultural studies, so fluid have the two histories been that there always remains a considerable body of work, a residue, which does not fit easily into the categorial system.

Here I shall adopt an alternative approach more in line with the analytic interests of this book, and certainly making no claims to be a comprehensive summary of the many points of intersection of feminism and cultural studies. We have already seen some of the ways in which the history of cultural studies crystallizes around differing forms of post-structuralism, in particular in the alternative positions found in *Screen* theory and in the work of the CCCS. These two schools of thought, while coinciding in their desire to make use of the concept of ideology as a central device in grasping the social role of culture, articulate that task, and the theories necessary for its successful application, in very different ways. For *Screen* theory the principal emphasis is on the process of subject positioning and, therefore, on the mechanisms (psychoanalytically conceived) through which that positioning is achieved within culture. Ideology here is predominantly a matter of the construction of subjects in texts and discourses. In the CCCS approach, ideology is viewed as an aspect of the process of securing hegemonic domination, and subject positioning is conceived as only one element in a more complex interaction between different components of culture. Relations between textual and real subjects, discursive systems and social agents, and culture and ideology, are much more socially negotiated here than in the apparent psychoanalytic determinism of classical *Screen* theory.

Of course, these 'snapshots' of the two traditions distort and simplify, freezing both *Screen* theory and CCCS work at one analytic moment in their development. There are many perils in that procedure (not least the tendency to remove complex and nuanced ideas from their conceptual context and thus make misunderstanding more likely) but the advantage for my present task lies in providing two coherent points of departure for understanding the entry of feminism into cultural studies. Inevitably, when feminism began to have an impact it did so in relation to prevailing theoretical positions, and it is possible to trace the subsequent intellectual history as a process of grappling with the consequences of attempting a specifically feminist reconstruction of these two cultural studies traditions. Accordingly, the discussion that follows falls into two sections. In the second I shall examine the kind of feminist cultural studies that emerged from engagement with the characteristic ideas represented in the work of the CCCS, as well as with the changes in those positions which, as we saw in Chapter 5, were already in process when feminism began to have its impact. McRobbie's work will serve as a useful initial focus here. In the first section, I shall examine the appropriation of subject-positioning theory for and by feminism as that was mediated through the extraordinarily influential essay by Laura Mulvey on 'Visual Pleasure and Narrative Cinema' (1975), as well as reflecting on some of the consequences of that for later considerations of 'spectatorship'. Inevitably, there is some convergence of interests between the two lines of argument, and I shall try to make that clearer toward the end of the chapter.

Subjects and spectators

It is some measure of the importance of Mulvey's argument that the literature is replete with attempts to summarize it and to draw out its implications. Interestingly, there is a good deal of variation in such accounts, partly, of course, because others have different theoretical axes to grind, but partly also because of difficulties with the text itself. For all its manifest influence and multiple reprinting, 'Visual Pleasure and Narrative Cinema' is a brief and densely argued essay which can give warrant to a range of readings. Where one interpreter might mainly pick up on its concern to influence feminist political-cultural practice, another might equally focus on its examination of gendered activity/passivity and the representation of women as spectacle, while yet another could attend to its characterization of the 'masculine' subject positioning intrinsic to classic narrative cinema. Over the years all these and numerous other positions have been attributed to Mulvey, most finding at least some justification in the original text.

Because of this marked variation, and before seeking to reconstruct her argument for my own ends, I shall first offer a summary account of Mulvey's position which sticks as closely as possible to the broad contours of the original essay. She begins by proclaiming her intention to use psychoanalytic theory as a political weapon, arguing that particular 'patterns of fascination' are to be found within individual subjects and the social formations which mould them, and that these serve to 'reinforce' the distinctive fascination of cinema. These subjects are constituted as male – she is careful to use the male third person singular – since 'the unconscious of patriarchal society has structured film form' (Mulvey, 1975: 6). At the heart of this process is phallocentrism which, borrowing from Freud and Lacan, she sees in terms of the central image of the castrated woman. In the space of one dense paragraph (*ibid*: 6–7) she offers a whole account of the paradoxical dependence of law, language, and the Symbolic on woman as castration threat. For feminists, she says (*ibid*: 7), this analysis 'gets us nearer to the roots of our oppression'.

How, then, does the unconscious structure forms of 'looking' in the cinema and the pleasures that we take? And how can we undermine that pleasure in the cause of feminist politics? The visual pleasures of the cinema are many, of course, but two of them in particular concern Mulvey. One she examines in terms of Freud's account of scopophilia, pleasurable looking, the voyeuristic satisfaction derived from observing a seemingly private world from a position of separation from it. The other (a rather different sense of 'look' is involved here) she conceptualizes in terms drawn from Lacan, trading on the resemblance of the cinema screen to the mirror in which the infant first encounters the subjective 'I'. Here the spectator's pleasure is that of narcissistic ego identification with the imaged figure. These two sources of pleasure are in tension in as much as the former separates the subject from on-screen object while the latter requires the subject to identify with that object. Furthermore, although looking produces pleasure in itself, when sexual difference is introduced what is actually seen may become threatening – woman as representation is encountered as both a source of voyeuristic pleasure and a threat of castration.

This can be seen in more detail in the way in which activity and passivity have been mapped on to male and female in film representation. The female figure is construed as spectacle in classic Hollywood, coded in terms of 'to-be-looked-at-ness', typically halting narrative action to facilitate the spectator's visually based erotic gratification. The active male spectator looks upon the passive female object. Meanwhile, in the narrative itself, the spectator finds an ego-ideal, an active, controlling male protagonist with whom he can identify, a figure who carries the look of the spectator into the world of the film. But there still remains a problem with the female figure. 'She also connotes something that the look continually circles around but disavows: her lack of a penis, implying a threat of castration and hence unpleasure' (*ibid*: 13). Thus, for all her presentation as erotic spectacle, the image of woman threatens the male unconscious with castration anxiety. Two main responses are possible. One involves investigation, demystification and punishment of the threatening figure, a strategy found in many film narratives which, thereby, neutralize the castration threat. The other resorts to fetishism, transmuting the represented woman by, typically, fetishizing female beauty in the cause of disavowing castration and thus reassuring the male spectator.

All this is captured in cinema through its characteristic play of looks. The looks of the camera and of the audience in classical narrative film are concealed by the codes of film form, subordinated to the looks of the characters as they relate to each other in the illusory film world. But this seamless illusion is endangered by woman as castration threat, and the suppression of the looks of the camera and of the audience ensure that this threat is defused. The camera's concealed look produces a verisimilitudinous world in which the spectator's ideal ego can control activity while the look of the audience is caught in a fetishistic denial of castration. If these pleasures are to be undermined, Mulvey argues, the looks of camera and audience must be freed from the codes that govern them. The visual pleasures of film are rooted in the patriarchal unconscious. In the cause of resisting patriarchy those pleasures must be destroyed.

This summarizes Mulvey's argument as she presents it. Now let me reconstruct her case with a view to pinning down more specifically what it involves. In effect, I shall conduct a kind of epistemological experiment, turning Mulvey's analysis around and viewing it as if it were what it is not: a formal, deductive attempt to explain a particular set of observed features of cinematic representation. This eases the task of unpacking the implicit structure of the theory but, hopefully, without sacrificing the main substance of Mulvey's views. Seen in this way, our point of departure lies not in a political claim about psychoanalytic theory (which is where Mulvey begins) but in an empirical claim about Hollywood cinema: that there are certain recurrent gender-related features that we can observe in classic Hollywood film. Specifically, this form of cinema: (1) presents narratives which are routinely controlled by male protagonists who (by a variety of means) subject female characters to their will; (2) represents women as erotic spectacle, as objects to be admired, arresting narrative progression to do so; and (3) fetishizes the female body, focusing upon different features (breasts, legs, hair, etc.) in different historical periods and contexts. Assuming we can agree that these are indeed widespread empirical features of Hollywood film – and it would be difficult not to do so – the task is to explain their presence, to answer the question: 'why is this so?'

Reconstructed in this way, the logic of Mulvey's approach is to take a certain body of psychoanalytic thought as foundational and therefore giving access to the patriarchal unconscious, derive from that theoretical material an account of the basic pleasures of looking which are (it is assumed) implicated in cinematic form, and go on to show how the satisfaction of these pleasures, in conjunction with a presumed need to disavow the castration threat, explains the observed phenomena. This chain of reasoning can usefully be given diagrammatic representation (see Figure 1).

Several structural features of the argument are immediately apparent from the figure. First, it depends entirely on prior acceptance of the apparatus of Freudian and Lacanian psychoanalytic theory *and* on a reading of that theory which presumes that it gives privileged access to 'the unconscious of patriarchy'. Secondly, the explanatory chain founded on the triplet of scopophilia, castration anxiety and narcissistic ego identification applies in two distinct areas (visual and narrative) and gives rise to two distinct kinds of claim in each: one founded on the need to disavow castration, the other on the specific form of pleasure involved (scopophilia, narcissistic ego identification). Thirdly, and related to that division, scopophilia and narcissistic ego identification are general psychic processes (that is, they refer to pleasures available to male *and* female) that are here given a

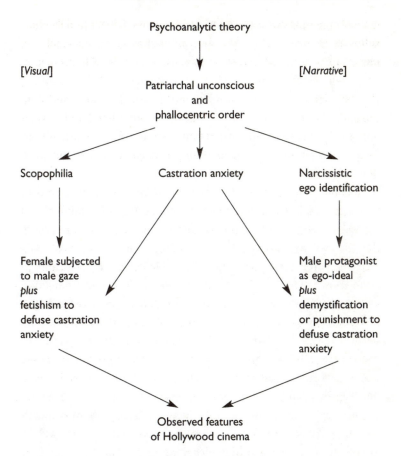

Figure 1 *'Visual Pleasure and Narrative Cinema' reconstructed*

male-upon-female gloss by the centrality of castration anxiety to the argument.

Viewed in this way, the effectiveness of Mulvey's case revolves around the strength of the explanation that she offers. Now, judgements of explanatory power are a function of three interlinked factors: the prior credibility of the explanatory theory; the logical consistency of the deductive links between the theory and the phenomena to be explained; and the relative strength of the explanation over other candidates. On the first of those three, judgement is not possible within the bounds of Mulvey's argument and remains controversial outside of it. The general efficacy of psychoanalytic theory is by no means self-evident or widely accepted, while the specific emphasis on castration anxiety in Mulvey's account would be questioned by many who might otherwise be positively disposed to psychoanalytic explanations. On the second criterion, as this reconstruction demonstrates, it is possible to trace a clear internal logic although it might be argued that some key terms of the theory remain ambiguous, not least those derived directly from Lacan. The third criterion is difficult to apply in the absence of specific competing explanations. However, there would seem to be a *prima facie* case, at least, for considering alternative explanations cast in terms of the social and historical development of patriarchal culture which would not necessarily resort to psychoanalytic concepts. In Mulvey, and in *Screen* theory more generally, however, such an alternative is not entertained and is, indeed, all but inconceivable. For although I have represented her argument here as only one candidate explanation of empirically observed features of Hollywood film, such an approach would be epistemologically alien to the *Screen* tradition within which she was working. In *Screen* theory, as we saw in Chapter 4, theories themselves construct their particular objects of analysis. Accordingly, Mulvey does not argue (as I have on her behalf) that such-and-such a feature of cinema can be explained by this (psychoanalytic) theory, although other (perhaps non-psychoanalytic) explanations are possible and may even be superior. That would be to employ an instrumental concept of 'theory', one in which competing theories are assessed in terms of their comparative empirical efficacy, and would be deemed unacceptable because of its links to an allegedly 'empiricist' problematic. Mulvey's approach, rather, *encloses* its topic within a theoretical system, seeking illumination by absorbing it into a pre-given framework. This is 'Theory' at work.

Leaving epistemological issues aside, the most remarked implication of her analysis is the predicative claim that the visual pleasures of classical Hollywood cinema presuppose a subject who takes pleasures that are essentially male. Once, that is, we have identified the central constitutive features of visual pleasure in Hollywood cinema, then the form itself is seen to interpellate a male subject. It is this aspect of her argument that precipitated much of the subsequent debate and, therefore, proved most influential in forming the terms in which 'spectatorship' came to prominence in (feminist) cultural studies. Most critical discussion (see, for example, the essays collected in Gamman and Marshment, 1988, and in *Screen*, 1992) revolved around the role of the female spectator. Where is she to place herself in relation to a form offering only male pleasures? Are there other (gendered) pleasures available? What of the male figure as an erotic object, or the female protagonist in film narratives? Surely gendered spectators can take up various subject positions in relation to Hollywood film?

These, and other more sweeping questions about the very utility of the psychoanalytic framework and its distinctive account of 'pleasure', ensured that a lively and sometimes fractious debate followed the publication of Mulvey's essay. Her position was widely disputed, variously adapted, and frequently misunderstood. Some of the misunderstandings, it must be said, were born of an overly literal reading of her claim about the 'masculine' character of the spectator's look, and as time passed Mulvey herself sought to restate her position in a more measured way. In 1981, in an 'Afterthought' that Gamman (1988: 191) not unfairly describes as only a 'slight revision' to the original argument, Mulvey still 'stands by' the main features of her position. But, while recognizing that the female spectator must perforce accept a male subject position and that such 'trans-sex identification is a *habit* that very easily becomes *second Nature*', she does go on to add the qualification that 'this Nature does not sit easily and shifts restlessly in its borrowed transvestite clothes' (Mulvey, 1990: 28). Some eight years after the 'Afterthought', that restlessness has been generalized to become, in retrospect, a constitutive part of the theory. 'I was using the term "masculine" in Freud's sense,' she writes of the original formulation, 'not referring to male in the sense of men in the audience, but to *the active element in the ambivalent sexuality of any individual*' (Mulvey, 1989: 73, my emphasis). 'Active'; 'ambivalent'; 'any individual'. Such terms signal a considerable change of emphasis, opening up the possibility of more complex negotiations between individual spectators and textually established subject positions: '[a]nyone, male or female, gay or straight, negotiates his or her own way into the pleasures of spectatorship, at face value, against the grain, or not at all' (*ibid*).

Whether or not this flexibility really was a key feature in Mulvey's original formulation remains a moot point; I am inclined to think not. It certainly was not how the original analysis was read, whether by those claiming to be in agreement with it or by those wishing to dispute one or another of its features. But, whatever the actual historical sequence, the prospect of spectator/textual-subject negotiations (rather than the textual determinism so prominent in the mainstream *Screen* theory tradition) did prove central to the whole debate. I shall not try to summarize this vast literature here, and, in any case, Mayne (1993) offers an excellent discussion. I shall only consider in the most general terms the four broad families of arguments that Mulvey's analysis provoked.

First, there were those who sought to show that while Hollywood film might indeed offer the pleasures that Mulvey identified, it also provided other pleasures which were at least as significant and which, therefore, required incorporation into any adequate theory. Furthermore, some argued, psychoanalytic concepts – even if appropriate in the Mulvey argument – were insufficient to the task of understanding the full range of such pleasures. Secondly, there were those who claimed that, whatever the distinctive character of the film text, spectators themselves were active agents who were capable of 'reading' their chosen cultural forms much more freely than the Mulvey position supposed. Women were not trapped in a male subject position; they were able to construct their own distinctive and often fluid relationships to texts produced within patriarchy. Again, in stronger versions of the argument, there was a tendency to doubt the psychoanalytic foundations upon which the original analysis rested which were thought to limit its capacity to comprehend active spectatorship. Thirdly, there were arguments already widely raised in relation to *Screen* theory, to the effect that texts simply should not be thought of as constituting monolithic subject positions; although they might indeed interpellate subjects, that process was far more complex than Mulvey's theory could countenance. And fourthly, some observed (as Mulvey herself appeared to do retrospectively) that spectators were not best viewed as gender-homogeneous; they brought a range of possibilities, some gendered, some not, to the reading situation.

What this critical discussion shared – and it was the great merit of Mulvey's work to put this so firmly on the feminist and cultural studies agendas – was a recognition that the nexus of relations between cultural 'text' and social 'reader', and between patriarchal culture and gendered agent, was not to be easily represented in a deterministic model. The degree of 'fit' between what Kuhn (1984)

calls the 'social audience' and the 'spectator', the former understood in social and economic terms, the latter as constructed
through signification, is a matter to be explored rather than presumed simply to flow from a text's constitution of subjectivity. This
is, as Kuhn suggests, part of the larger challenge of grappling with
text/context relations, a challenge that has continued to inform
subsequent theories of spectatorship. Mayne (1993: 42–43) summarizes this history in terms of a series of alternative models
posed against 'institutional' or 'apparatus' theories of the kind represented by Mulvey. There are 'empirical models', of which she
identifies the cognitive and ethnographic variations, and which ask
how viewers actually respond to texts; 'historical models', which
seek to understand spectatorship as historically and culturally specific; and, of course, the various counter-views developed in the
course of the feminist debate precipitated by Mulvey's paper. To
better grasp these developments requires us to examine the
second area in which feminism has had a significant impact on cultural studies theory.

Women's culture

Whereas most commentators would agree that the Mulvey essay
is a *locus classicus* for the impact of feminist thinking on the *Screen*
theory strand of cultural studies, it is not possible to find a single
text to exemplify the conjunction of feminism with the second of
my two cultural studies traditions. This is hardly surprising. So
influential was 'Visual Pleasure and Narrative Cinema' that it
turned the then emergent subject-positioning theory irrevocably
toward feminist issues, much extended the diffusion of psychoanalytic ideas throughout cultural studies, and placed gendered
spectatorship firmly at the centre of discussion. It is rare for one

contribution to have such a remarkable effect. To understand what happened to the CCCS-mediated version of post-structuralism, however, we will need to cast our net more widely. We can usefully begin this task by looking at aspects of the thinking of one feminist scholar, Angela McRobbie, who worked initially within the CCCS and whose changing concerns reflect the larger movement of feminist-influenced cultural studies. McRobbie has not been as influential as Mulvey, but she has followed a path that we can take to typify more general theoretical and methodological trends.

Let us begin with her essay 'Working class girls and the culture of femininity' in the CCCS Women's Studies Group volume, *Women Take Issue*, which catches well the intellectual tenor of the times (McRobbie, 1978). The essay is based on her CCCS MA thesis of the same title, in which she explored various aspects of the lifestyle and culture of a group of teenage girls who were members of a local youth club. In many respects this work falls firmly within the prevailing tradition of CCCS subculture studies (see Hall and Jefferson, 1976), using a range of methods – participant observation, interviews, diaries, questionnaires, etc. – to assemble a body of data about the girls' distinctive culture. McRobbie draws on the class aspects of CCCS subculture theory, concerning herself with the 'interpellation' of the girls as class subjects and asking 'how do the effects of this positioning find expression at the level of a developing class identity?' (McRobbie, 1978: 100). Aspects of her argument are akin to that advanced by Willis (1977) in one of the best known CCCS ethnographic studies, in as much as, like Willis' 'lads', these girls are victims of their own anti-school culture: 'it is their own culture which itself is the most effective agent of social control for girls' (McRobbie, 1978: 104).

For all its family resemblance to the prevailing CCCS subculture tradition, however, McRobbie's analysis is also strongly inflected with feminism. Feminist interventions in the sociology of the 1970s characteristically (and rightly) observed that women were rendered invisible in much research, concepts of gender being largely absent from sociological theory. McRobbie is explicitly concerned to 'redress this balance' in the area of youth studies by examining the ways in which the culture of femininity is constituted and the impact it has had on the girls' lives. And while class remains for her the centrally significant reference point that it was for contemporary CCCS work, in itself she considers it insufficient for a full understanding of the girls' social situation. 'The culture of adolescent working class girls can be seen as a response to the material limitations imposed on them as a result of their class position, but also as an index of, and response to their sexual oppression as women' (*ibid*: 108). Then, invoking a tension between positive and negative aspects of women's culture that was to become much more prominent in later feminist cultural studies, she adds that the girls 'are both saved by and locked within the culture of femininity'.

Thus far, then, we can see feminism seeking to: (a) combat the 'invisibility' of women in sociological and cultural studies research; (b) incorporate gender into prevailing theoretical models, especially those of the marxist tradition; and (c) begin to address the tension between a positive appreciation of women's distinctive culture and its role in their continuing oppression. Subsequent feminist cultural studies progressed along all these lines. McRobbie herself continued to mount a critique of subculture research in the late 1970s (see Chapters 1 and 2 in McRobbie, 1991a) taking to task both Willis (1977) and Hebdige (1979) for their failure to introduce gender into their analyses. More importantly, as she herself observes (McRobbie, 1991a: xvii), her work 'turned away from subcultures to the terrain of domestic life', the social context that she deemed most appropriate for understanding female youth culture. In making this move and examining the ways in which young girls interact to form a distinctive culture, she is at one level focusing upon the ideology of patriarchy in action, but at another she also recognizes the possibility of a form of resistance that turns teenybopper culture 'into a site of active feminine identity' (*ibid*: 14).

In pursuit of this aspect of the formation of teenage girls' identity, McRobbie turned her attention to the typical cultural texts of teenage femininity, most notably the hugely popular girls' magazine *Jackie*. In her original discussion – dating from the mid-1970s – she embarks on what she describes (1991a: 81–82) as 'a systematic critique of *Jackie* as a system of messages, a signifying system and a bearer of a certain ideology, an ideology which deals with the construction of teenage femininity'. In doing that, of course, she remains within the theoretical presuppositions of CCCS textual analysis of the time, with its concern to reveal the ideological mechanisms through which hegemony is secured. Through the magazines, she argues, 'teenage girls are subjected to an explicit attempt to win consent to the dominant order – in terms of femininity, leisure and consumption' (*ibid*: 87). The model is one of ideology 'pushing' the girls in specific directions, operating through the 'codes' that she identifies: those of romance, personal/domestic life, fashion and beauty, and pop music. Overall, she concludes, '*Jackie* presents "romantic individualism" as the ethos *par excellence* of the teenage girl' (*ibid*: 131).

Typically for the period, most of this analysis revolves around the texts themselves, on the assumption that their repeated absorption – McRobbie talks about this 'powerful' discourse being 'absorbed' by its readers – has hegemonic consequences. Only at the very end of her discussion (*ibid*: 132) does she note that it is also important to know 'how girls read *Jackie* and encounter its ideological force'. This is not just a reflection of the wider theoretical doubts then emerging about 'top-down' ideology-based models of culture, but also a manifestation of the growing feminist concern to document women's 'lived experience'. This was always apparent in the ethnographic aspect of McRobbie's studies of young girls' culture, but in the 1980s – as in both cultural studies and feminism more generally – it was to grow in significance. When McRobbie returned to girls' magazines at the end of the 1980s, a whole new literature had developed. Not only on women's magazines and romantic fiction, which were now 'recognized as key cultural forms reflective of distinctively feminine pleasures' (*ibid*: 135), but also in the developing fields of reception studies and theories of readership. In this context it is notable that, as well as recognizing the decline of romance as a central topic in the 1980s magazines, McRobbie no longer views the discourse as ideologically constraining to the degree that she did in the earlier study. Times had changed, empirically and theoretically.

In due course these changes would see the study of culture 'quite dramatically transformed as questions of modernity and postmodernity [have] replaced the more familiar concepts of ideology and hegemony' (McRobbie, 1991b: 1). But that is a topic for the next chapter. Here I am more concerned to examine the distinctively feminist element in the 1980s decline of top-down, textually oriented theories. We have seen in the pattern of McRobbie's work how an initial determination to render women visible in cultural studies and sociology progressed through a critique of existing work toward a comprehensive 'gendering' of theory. This was succeeded by an increasingly distinctive focus on women's culture, a focus which attended appreciatively to forms of culture previously neglected or denigrated yet retained varying degrees of commitment to the view that 'female forms' were a vital part of the ideological apparatus of patriarchal domination. This was to be seen especially in the studies of soap opera (Dyer *et al.*, 1981; Hobson, 1982; Ang, 1985; Geraghty, 1991) and romantic fiction (Modleski, 1982; Radway, 1987) that became so prominent in 1980s cultural studies. Several themes run through this work, four of which will be examined here: ideology; gendered pleasure; readership; and identity. All four interrelate, of course, so this division is somewhat artificial, if convenient.

Let us begin with ideology, at the start of the 1980s still the touchstone for so much of cultural studies. In attending to women's culture and inquiring about the pleasures that women took from this material, feminist scholars were obliged to question the conventional designation of such texts as straightforward carriers of patriarchal ideology. In one of the earliest explorations of the issue in relation to soap opera, Terry Lovell (1981: 50–51) seeks to supplement conventional views of ideology by recognizing the distinctive uses that women may make of the form:

> *Coronation Street* offers its women viewers certain 'structures of feeling' which are prevalent in our society, and which are only partially recognised in the normative patriarchal order. It offers women a validation and celebration of those interests and concerns which are seen as properly theirs within the social world they inhabit. Soap opera may be the opium of masses of women, but . . . it may also be . . . a context in which women can ambiguously express *both* good-humoured acceptance of their oppression *and* recognition of that oppression and some equally good-humoured protest against it.

In posing the issue in this way, Lovell is recognizing that ideology and pleasure are not straightforwardly related. The interface between them, as she puts it, 'is always and necessarily an irregular one' (*ibid*: 48). Of course, pleasures are crucial to the ways in which cultural forms serve ideological functions, but to uncover the ideology apparently conveyed in a text is to say little or nothing

about the pleasures that it provides. Hence her resort to Williams'
expression 'structures of feeling' in an attempt to catch those
elements of *Coronation Street* that are pleasurable to women while
standing in an ambiguous, even contradictory, relation to patriarchal ideology.

This tension between the demands of an approach focused upon
ideology and those grounded in the recognition that women make
active use of 'their own' cultural artefacts increasingly pervades
1980s work. On romantic fiction, for example, while conceding that
such material may be ideological in as much as it 'inoculates' its
readers against some of the 'evils of sexist society', Modleski (1982:
43) makes much the same point as Lovell. 'Instead of exploring the
possibility that romances, while serving to keep women in their
place, may at the same time be concerned with real female problems, analysts of women's romances have generally seen the
fantasy embodied in romantic fiction as evidence of female
"masochism" or as a simple reflection of the dominant masculine
ideology' (*ibid*: 37–38). Similarly, Radway (1987: 14–15) suggests
that, even after extensive research, she is still not able to untangle
the answers to a crucial pair of questions: 'Does the romance's
endless rediscovery of the virtues of a passive female sexuality
merely stitch the reader ever more resolutely into the fabric of
patriarchal culture? Or, alternatively, does the satisfaction a reader
derives from the act of reading itself, an act she chooses, often in
explicit defiance of others' opposition, lead to a new sense of
strength and independence?' So, while there does remain wide
recognition that women's popular culture may indeed help to reconcile women to patriarchal social forms – though Radway's (1987:
217) point is well made, that direct evidence is lacking to support
this claim – there is also a clear and growing desire to engage
more positively with the ways in which these cultural forms are
pleasurable to their female audience.

This issue of gendered pleasure is the second of my four themes. If women are seen to respond positively to certain cultural forms, such as soap opera and romances, what is it about those forms which makes them gender specific in their appeal? Much of the 1980s literature revolves around this question, and two kinds of answers are proposed. One works by identifying particular features of the texts under consideration which, by common consent, might be expected to appeal to women. The other pushes the question somewhat further, advancing general theories as to why the pleasures provided should be characteristically female. Theoretically, of course, the latter is essential to the former – 'common consent' on what constitutes women's pleasure is always in need of explanation and theorizing – and much-remarked textual features (for example strong female characters in soap opera) only appear to have self-evident gender appeal because of 'commonsense' assumptions we make about gendered pleasure. Furthermore, without such theorization there is always a risk of circularity, of presupposing that because some form of culture is seen as a 'women's genre' it necessarily caters to gender-specific needs and desires.

I shall not examine theories of gendered pleasure in any detail here. The important thing to note for present purposes is that, whatever the specifics of these theories, they invariably postulate a distinctive gendered identity (my third theme) from which emerge the needs, tastes and desires in which pleasure is grounded. In the older strong ideology models, gender identity is itself a product of patriarchal ideology, such that culture both forms women's needs and then goes on to satisfy them. In this way patriarchal society finds its own means to preserve the status quo. But where the constraints of traditional ideology models are loosened – as they are increasingly in feminist cultural studies – other sources are posed for the formation of gendered identity.

Both Modleski and Radway, for example, make use of Chodorow's (1978) psychoanalytic account of the significance of the mother–daughter relationship in constituting the female unconscious. Modleski (1982: 73–74, 98–100) uses it to explore aspects of the appeal of both Gothic novels and soap operas, while Radway (1987: 12–14, 135–140) invokes Chodorow's views on the female need for nurturance in explaining the appeal of romantic fiction. Unlike the use of Lacan in *Screen* theory, however, Chodorow's work is not employed by these scholars as a degree zero theory of identity formation. It features, rather, as one aspect of the theoretical apparatus necessary to understand the impact of gender identity on the provision of textual pleasures. This has not prevented charges of illicit essentialism being laid at the door of those who seek to isolate a distinct gender identity, but, by and large, the fact that considerations of identity have been only one element in a larger account of readership has mitigated the potential effects of such essentialism.

In part, this has been because the process of 'reading' cultural texts has been given more attention throughout cultural studies over the past decade. The need to understand how agents actually read the (ideological) texts supplied by their culture was becoming increasingly apparent in both the *Screen* theory and CCCS traditions by the early 1980s, an emphasis which was developing quite independent of any feminist intervention. However, post-CCCS feminist cultural studies did lend considerable impetus to this process in seeking to document and understand the reading practices of women in relation to female cultural forms. Quite early on McRobbie, as we have already seen, was fully aware of the need to examine how her research subjects actually responded to the ideological baggage of *Jackie*, even if she did not herself pursue that line of research.

Others in the 1980s were more direct. Hobson (1982: 105–136), in her CCCS-originated study of the soap opera *Crossroads*, conducted interviews and recorded 'unstructured conversations' with the women viewers of the programme. Although she was not concerned with the reading process as such – at least, not in the way that some later researchers would be – she did begin to document significant aspects of the ways in which soap operas were watched. Ang (1985), too, examined viewers' responses, this time to *Dallas* and via letters solicited from fans, using this material as a basis for discussing the familiar concerns of ideology, pleasure, and women viewers. And Radway (1987) confronted the reading process head on in her study of a group of romance readers united in their common status as customers of a particular bookshop. In her introduction to the English edition – the book was first published in the USA three years earlier, in 1984 – she sees her research as falling firmly into a then growing tradition of 'ethnographic' studies of readership, grounded in the claim that 'empirically-based ethnographies of reading should replace *all* intuitively conducted interpretation in cultural study, precisely because such empiricism would guarantee a more *accurate* description of what a book meant to a given audience' (*ibid*: 5). Of course, there is nothing uniquely feminist about that claim. Nevertheless, such work was frequently motivated by a feminist concern to appreciate the full complexity of women's reading practices in relation to cultural forms often demeaned as crass escapism or patriarchal propaganda. No doubt the turn to an ethnographic interest in readership would have found expression in cultural studies with or without feminism. In the event, however, feminist interest in the domestic context, in previously under-analysed cultural forms, and in the tension between ideological constraint and women's pleasure, was crucial in shaping subsequent developments.

Gender and cultural studies

How, then, can we summarize the effect of feminist sensibilities on the cultural studies project? First of all, at a practical level feminism made women 'visible' to cultural studies, just as it did in so many of the social sciences and humanities. The importance of that is not to be underestimated. However prominent a topic of study women may be today, it is worth recalling quite how invisible they were before feminism made its presence felt. The sociology into which I was educated in the first half of the 1960s, for example, paid little attention to women, except in very specific areas and in very limited ways, and this continued to be the case even as sociology garnered its reputation for political radicalism as the decade progressed. In addition to the practical achievement of pushing women into the foreground of scholarly attention, feminism also promoted the cause of gender theory. To see the significance of women as a topic of study was also to recognize that gender was a much neglected, but nevertheless fundamental, feature of all social and cultural analysis. In cultural studies this meant both examining gendered culture, cultural products that were differentially associated with men and women, and examining gender *in* culture. Although the former has been crucial – witness the studies of women's cultural forms considered in the last section – it is arguable that the diffusion of a gender awareness throughout the emerging theories and methods of cultural studies has finally had the more pervasive influence.

Turning, therefore, to these more theoretical matters, this chapter's discussion suggests three broad areas in which feminism has had a lasting impact on the practice of cultural studies: theories of spectatorship; theories of the interrelation of ideology, reading and resistance; theories of (gendered) pleasure and (gender) identity. The first of the three emerges from the gendered spectatorship debate. As we have seen, the terms in which this topic came to the fore derived from Mulvey's work, whether staying broadly within its framework or reacting against it. The idea that texts, cultural forms, and even whole discourses might construct their users as gendered subjects proved helpfully provocative, immediately raising two kinds of general questions about spectatorship. What features of cultural artefacts allow them to produce certain kinds of gendered response? What is it about gendered individuals that leads them to respond in distinctive ways? In approaching the first question, researchers drew upon the established traditions of post-structuralist textual analysis to elucidate the part played by gender and patriarchy in forming processes of signification. At its simplest this led to analyses of the 'images of women' type, uncovering the (stereotypical) ways in which women were represented in culture. But such work was rapidly overtaken by a more far-reaching examination of the terms of signification itself, a form of theorizing typified by Mulvey's account of the patriarchal character of classical Hollywood discourse. At the same time, this analysis of textual systems required some way of conceptualizing the gendered character of individual responses, not simply to deal with the problem posed for a female audience faced with Mulvey's 'male' subject position, but also to reconcile the social and historical subject with that constructed textually.

As it did more generally in 1980s cultural studies, this tension between 'real' and 'textual' subjects fed into most other significant developments. So in the second of my areas of feminist influence, the issues were the familiar ones of the relations between ideology, the process of 'reading', and the potential for political and cultural resistance, but given a distinctive feminist twist. If the texts of popular culture were imbued with patriarchal ideology, both in their form and their content, was there any possibility of resisting the force of this ideology by, among other methods, reading against the grain? Much feminist political practice was committed to this strategy, arising in considerable part from the doctrine that the 'personal is political'. This crystallized in an acute form the evident contradictions between, on the one hand, a view that recognized the enormous power of patriarchal ideology and, on the other, a political commitment to resisting that power wherever it was manifest. In dealing with this contradiction, feminist researchers, whether concerned to defend women's cultural forms such as soap opera and romances or to raise more general questions of female spectatorship, lent considerable impetus to those arguing for a more active conception of readership in cultural studies. The strong ideology theories of the 1970s were already facing difficulties by the end of that decade; feminist work of the 1980s greatly accelerated their decline.

This growing focus on the nature and activity of gendered 'readers' foregrounded the interrelated topics of the constitution of gendered pleasure and, more generally, gender identity. This, too, was both influenced by and influential upon broader trends in cultural studies. The pleasures afforded by culture had been systematically neglected in both main cultural studies traditions. So concerned had analysts been to demonstrate the ideological power of texts that they had all but forgotten that such power was dependent on readers taking pleasure from those texts in the first place. The terms of post-structuralism – including, it should be said, the very general concepts of *plaisir* and *jouissance* so often borrowed from Barthes – afforded little leverage to those wanting to understand the specifics of the pleasures readers took from texts. One response to that limitation was empirically to examine the process of reading itself, with a view to developing a more detailed sense of what was involved. The so-called 'ethnographic turn' in cultural studies was central to this project, a shift in which feminist research played a crucial part. A second, less empirically focused response involved turning to theories of identity in an attempt to delineate the fundamental features of gender in which pleasures were grounded. Here psychoanalytic concepts became central, derived not only from the Lacanian 'structural psychoanalysis' already pervading the *Screen* theory tradition, but also from other more clearly feminist revisions of Freud such as that found in Chodorow's work.

This is perhaps the most tangled area of feminist influence on cultural studies theory. The use of psychoanalytic theory has remained controversial within feminism, as elsewhere, although it is probably fair to say that it has gained much wider acceptance since Mitchell (1974: xv) began her pioneering defence with the blunt observation that '[t]he greater part of the feminist movement has identified Freud as the enemy'. Happily this history is beyond my scope here, other than to observe that – whatever one's judgement on the virtues and failings of psychoanalytic theory itself – as a loose framework of concepts it has been of considerable significance in shaping the growth of feminist cultural studies. In the course of that, inevitably, charges of gender essentialism, over-determinism and reductionism have been levelled at its supporters, sometimes for good reason. In consequence, alternative ways of approaching identity and gender have emerged, more sensitive to variations in social and cultural context, as recent 'postmodern' forms of feminist cultural studies have served to suggest. Where they will lead remains to be seen. But at the most general theoretical level it is important to recognize that, on top of all the specific contributions that feminism has made to cultural studies, it has also played a crucial role in the theoretical and methodological movement away from the deterministic post-structuralism of the 1970s and toward the relativistic postmodernism of the 1990s. It is to mapping that shift that we now turn.

7 *The Rise of the Reader*

The cultural studies inheritance from structuralism was not simply a matter of new terminology, a methodological focus on signification, and a desire to theorize *langue* wherever it might be found. Structuralism and the various post-structuralisms were marked by a conceptual tension that runs like an undercurrent through the cultural studies project. On the one hand, structuralists and post-structuralists were committed to understanding the constraints imposed by structures of whatever kind. But on the other hand, as Saussure had before them, they also recognized the social relativity of semiotic systems, their inbuilt potential for polysemy, and the inventive capacities of the social agents who made creative use of them. In the terms that I borrowed from Giddens (1984) in Chapter 3, structuralism had the potential to see culture as both constraining and enabling. Culture stores and delivers the resources that social agents utilize in making their world make sense, and in that respect sets limits, defines terms, constrains the character of social life. But cultures are also complex, contradictory and ambiguous, open to constant reconstruction by users who are, by their very nature, active manipulators of cultural materials. Culture may indeed be a reservoir on which we draw to constitute social activity; but it also reflects and refracts that activity in an ongoing circle of production and reproduction.

In the first two decades of cultural studies' growth, it was the constraining aspects of culture that were to the analytic fore. In part that was a consequence of the contingent connection forged between various forms of 'new' marxism and the emergent cultural studies of the late 1960s, but it also reflected structuralism's own conceptual imperatives. Without first establishing the systematic structuring capacities of semiotic systems one could not hope to go on to examine those systems in use, and the codes through which *langue* functioned had to be understood before it was possible to approach questions of diversity and polysemy in *parole*. Accordingly, a 'top-down' approach to culture, one in which social agents were largely on the receiving end of cultural determination, was always the most likely initial model in structuralist-influenced cultural studies. Add to that a *marxisant* concern with the role of ideology in sustaining capitalist social and economic structures, and we find the distinctive forms of post-structuralism that characterize the theoretical traditions associated with *Screen* theory and the CCCS. In these traditions, as they were initially formulated at least, culture is all but exhausted by its ideological function.

This reduction of culture to ideology, and the concomitant emphasis on its presumed power to constrain and control individuals, was also apparent in the first feminist interventions in cultural studies, particularly in their concern to document patriarchal ideology in action. However, as we saw in the last chapter, the underlying tension between structural constraint and active agency becomes increasingly prominent in feminist cultural studies, not least because the evident pleasures afforded to women by 'women's culture' were unintelligible within the terms of conventional ideology theories – they could only be dismissed as 'false consciousness'. Hence feminism's ongoing interest in such topics as pleasure, active readership, and constructive polysemy. But these are not only gender issues; they are also general aspects of the relation between human agency and culture, aspects that the main traditions of cultural studies had neglected in their desire to focus upon culture's capacity to constrain. In response to such neglect, the 1980s and 1990s have seen the theoretical pendulum swing away from top-down, dominant ideology models and toward a rather more open concern with culture's relation to active agency.

These changes have provoked claims that there is an emerging 'paradigm crisis' in cultural studies, and it is this topic that forms the focus for this chapter. I shall examine the changing state of cultural studies theory and method as it is embodied in two main developments, before going on to make some observations about the 'crisis'. Both developments derive from what is sometimes described as a postmodern attempt to reconceptualize media audiences as more diverse and active contributors to processes of interpretation and communication. The first is particularly concerned to document that 'activity' as it is found in natural social settings, tending to make use of a variety of methodologies that have been loosely – perhaps too loosely – categorized as 'ethnographic'. The second development revolves around the emergence of a kind of celebratory and allegedly uncritical semiotics of popular culture, a form of so-called 'cultural populism' that has provoked considerable debate. The two developments are not unrelated, but they are sufficiently different in their emphases to merit separate treatment here.

Audience ethnography

We have already seen in general terms how the issue of active readership edged to the fore in the later stages of both *Screen* theory's account of subject positioning and the CCCS' use of the encoding/decoding model. Neither approach proved able to deal satisfactorily with the nexus of relations between culture, text and reader. Lacking concepts appropriate to the task they tended to submerge the nascent 'active reader' in models that prioritized determination by, respectively, psychoanalytic processes securing the subject or socio-political processes securing hegemony. It is not that exponents of either view were unaware of these limitations. It is, rather, that the key terms with which they theorized culture and communication were dualistic, inviting analyses in terms of the dominance of structures over specific social agents, or, in principle if not in practice, vice versa.

I shall return to the perils of theoretical dualism later. For the present it is necessary to get some sense of how reaction against these views in the 1980s precipitated an alternative approach to readership, a topic I shall approach by first considering aspects of David Morley's work in the years following the *Nationwide* study. In Chapter 5 we saw some of the ways in which the CCCS study of *Nationwide* sought to apply the encoding/decoding model, which was already a step toward an active audience conception in comparison with older traditions of media research. It is now commonplace to suggest that this study, especially in its most audience-oriented component (Morley, 1980b), demonstrated the inherent limitations of the encoding/decoding model, and, notwithstanding Morley's (1992: 10–12) own inclination to dissent from this judgement, there is no doubt that it marks an initial move away from the terms of the classic CCCS position. The *Nationwide* study, as Morley suggests, may indeed have been retrospectively misrepresented by Fiske (1987) and Turner (1990) for example, but this does not mean that they are wrong in seeing it as an early sign of what was to become a marked conceptual shift.

That shift is certainly apparent in Morley's next study, *Family*

Television (Morley, 1986: 14), where, as he puts it himself, 'my focus of interest had thus shifted from the analysis of the pattern of differential audience "readings" of particular programme materials [the *Nationwide* study] to the analysis of the domestic viewing context itself – as the framework within which "readings" of programmes are ordinarily made'. By interviewing 18 families (initially parents, and then their children as well) he hoped to develop an understanding of how television was viewed and used in the domestic setting that forms its 'natural' viewing environment. In the event, if there is a single aspect that is foregrounded in this research, it is gender and the ways in which gender-based power manifests itself in the routine practices of television viewing: 'the one structural principle working across all the families interviewed is that of gender' (*ibid*: 146). For all its evident significance, however, that is not the aspect to which I wish to draw attention here. My concern is more with Morley's admirable theoretical intent 'to formulate a position from which we can see the person actively producing meanings from the restricted range of cultural resources which his or her structural position has allowed them access to' (*ibid*: 43).

Now it is not clear to me – nor, to be fair, is it claimed by Morley (1992: 59–60) – that *Family Television* actually provides us with this sort of access to processes of meaning production in a structuring context. Readers of the interview accounts may receive glimmers of such insight, but only by constructing their own theoretical analyses in the course of reading the material. Apart from gender, which is afforded a separate discussion, there is no systematic account of 'the restricted range of cultural resources' employed by the interviewees in constructing meaning. I do not intend that observation as a strong criticism; to draw out such processes from detailed interview data is a formidable challenge. But it does lead me to two general observations about this and other similarly disposed research. First, even today we lack the theoretical resources to implement Morley's project of relating active meaning production to the structuring restrictions imposed by culture, although growing interest in Bourdieu's (1977, 1986) work in the 1990s may go some way toward remedying that lack. Secondly, as we know from other areas of sociology, there is a methodological risk with this kind of qualitative research that the provision of 'rich description' (Geertz, 1973) comes to substitute for analysis; presentation of the 'ethnographic' material becomes an end in itself. Neither of these difficulties is insuperable, nor do they constitute reasons for not pursuing the project that Morley proposes. But they do suggest the need for more in the way of theoretical and methodological reflection.

Let us begin that process with an apparently straightforward methodological question: in what senses is Morley's and other similar audience research appropriately described as 'ethnography'? If one were to adopt a strict definition of the kind that used to be accepted in, say, social and cultural anthropology, then the work of Morley or Ang (1985) or Buckingham (1987) or Gray (1992) or Radway (1987), whatever its many virtues, would hardly count as ethnographic. The classical ethnographic project required extensive participant observation fieldwork with a view to the researcher's total immersion in the social and cultural world of the subjects. In consequence of this immersion, sometimes over a period of years, the ethnographer would then generate a thoroughgoing description of the system. The resulting account was naturalistic and holistic: the former in its assumption that it was possible to 'get inside' the culture and understand it from its participants' point of view; the latter in the ambition to offer an account of it as a whole system of social interaction. Some of that ambition does survive in modern audience research. Most of these researchers would wish to see the researched world from their subjects' points of view and, in so doing, understand social activity in its context. But that would be true also of symbolic interactionism, or, indeed, any of the many alternative research methodologies that emerged in 1970s sociology and cast themselves in broadly 'phenomenological' terms.

Compared with the classical form, then, what is missing from the recent audience research version of 'ethnography' is extended participant observation. As Moores (1993: 33) observes of Lull (1980): 'his project is one of the few audience ethnographies to have relied chiefly on long periods of participant observation', a strategy Lull adopted to minimize disruption caused by the investigator and thence allow a fuller appreciation of the role of everyday family activities. In contrast, most audience research in the 'ethnographic' tradition has utilized open-ended and semi-structured interview techniques rather than participant observation, sometimes with individuals, sometimes with groups. In this respect, a more appropriate term for this style of inquiry would be 'qualitative audience research', which catches its distinctiveness more effectively than does 'ethnography'. However, the usage is widely established by now, and even recent writers on 'ethnography' more generally, such as Hammersley (1992: 8), tend to use the term as interchangeable with 'qualitative method'. While it is unfortunate to lose the holistic sense conveyed in the expression *'an* ethnography', provided that no one assumes that 'audience ethnography' is distinguished by application of systematic participant observation, then the label will make little difference.

What does make a difference is the researcher's understanding of the purpose of such research and of the epistemology that the methodological practice presupposes, and here it *is* vital to recognize the ways in which audience ethnographies depart from the classic naturalist-empiricist model. Morley (1992: 183) has suggested that the ethnographic approach to communication 'rests on an ability to understand how social actors themselves define and understand their own communication practices – their decisions, their choices and the consequences of both for their daily lives and their subsequent actions – as well as on the ability of the researcher to bring into the analysis (and even offer his or her subjects) the benefits of more structural considerations'. In its first part, this passage could represent any *Verstehen*-inclined research strategy, any attempt to remain true to the character of actors' experiences of everyday life, so it is not surprising to find Morley invoking the father of phenomenological sociology, Alfred Schutz, a page or two later. In its second part, however, a more distinctive claim is being made about the importance of incorporating 'structural considerations'. That immediately begs the question of what conceptual materials such structural considerations are composed, which, in turn, requires the 'ethnographer' to lay out the theory of structure through which these phenomena will be identified. Structures do not identify themselves; they require conceptual framing. Morley's formulation clearly assumes that these concepts are brought to the analysis by the researcher – they do not simply emerge inductively from the phenomenal account.

Two kinds of claim are being made here. One supposes that it is both possible and desirable to understand audience activity from within and to describe that activity in its own terms. The other requires that such 'ethnographic' description be related to some model of structure that is used to (re)interpret patterns of activity in a larger socio-cultural context. Morley's use of gender in *Family Television* is presumably an instance of such interpretation, but it remains untheorized in its relation to other aspects of the structuring environment. Of course, a radically phenomenological position would anyway deny the validity and possibility of the second structuring moment of Morley's project, accepting only accounts cast in the terms provided by the social agents involved.

Few audience ethnographers have explicitly adopted such a strict epistemology, however, although rather more may have fallen into it by default in as much as they have found themselves focusing upon the richness of their descriptive material at the expense of any systematic attempt to relate it to the larger structures which are putatively involved.

There is a lengthy history of debate over this issue in sociology where, especially since the 1970s, the impact of phenomenologically inclined thinking has been considerable. When the mainstream consensus collapsed in sociology in the late 1960s, it did so in part for epistemological reasons. The previously well established commitment to 'scientific sociology' and a hypothetico-deductive model of scientific inquiry lost credibility, partly because it had simply not delivered the goods, and partly because it faced a growing barrage of conventionalist and relativist criticism within the philosophy of science. The emerging alternatives resisted the abstraction of traditional sociological theory, along with its concern with macroscopic patterns of structural determination, the alleged scientism of large-scale quantitative research, and many of the more structural concepts that had become established in the course of the discipline's twentieth-century development. Schools of thought arose that were exclusively focused upon microscopic aspects of social life, using qualitative methods to interpret processes of meaningful interaction, and largely disregarding questions about the effectivity of social structure. To document the richness and complexity of social interaction became a sufficient goal in itself.

Any reader of modern audience ethnographies will recognize that description, and some of the reasons for the equivalent move in cultural studies are similar to those that gave rise to sociology's 1970s crisis and the 'perspectival wars' that followed. As we have seen, the main post-structuralist traditions in cultural studies had undervalued detailed empirical research, often simply dismissing it as indefensibly empiricist. Yet it had become increasingly apparent that any serious attempt to grapple with the relation between the structuring capacities of cultural texts and the agency of readers needed to understand processes of reading in actual social and historical contexts. Research into audiences, however, had been the province of the mass communications research tradition which was itself dominated by a scientistic model of inquiry and by quantitative methods. It is hardly surprising, then, that when cultural studies came to embrace empirical research into audiences it did so in qualitative and largely microscopic terms, and even though Morley's formulation of the project does invoke 'structural considerations', audience ethnographies thus far have done little to realise that ambition, either conceptually or empirically.

Methodological debate has therefore been less about the challenge of incorporating a conjoint understanding of structure and agency – arguably the first requirement for those concerned to elucidate text–reader relations – than about the inevitable partiality of ethnographic accounts and their relation to political practice. These are important issues, of course, and their discussion in the cultural studies literature has been deeply influenced by the methodological 'crisis' in anthropological thought of recent years (Clifford and Marcus, 1986; James *et al.*, 1997). Central to this debate has been the recognition that '[e]thnographic truths are thus inherently *partial*' (Clifford and Marcus, 1986: 7) – as are, one might say, all putative empirical truths – a view which, in a cultural studies context, leads swiftly on to a series of questions about what it is that ethnographic accounts actually represent, how they relate to other representations offered by audience members or other observers, what political role they might play in a critical cultural studies, in what forms they should be given expression, and whether and how the reflexivity of the ethnographer should be incorporated within the research (cf. Ang, 1996). The underlying threads here are relativism and constructivism: the relativism of knowledge claims and the consequent risk of an endless spiral of irreconcilable accounts, constructed from the various points of view of participants and observers, and undermining the possibility of any meaningful intervention in, or generalized understanding of, culture in society.

Conventionalist epistemologies always risk this paralysis in which the impossibility of certainty leads to a contextualist and reflexive retreat from making any claims at all. The solution, if solution it be, is to recognize that the partiality of truth claims, and the potential multiplicity of accounts of social process, do not necessitate our discarding all forms of epistemological realism. By this I do not mean that we should return to a version of simple ethnographic realism in which the ethnographer unproblematically represents the real world of the researched. Rather, with Hammersley (1992: 50) we should accept that '[w]e can maintain belief in the existence of phenomena independent of our claims about them, and in their knowability, without assuming that we can have unmediated contact with them and therefore that we can know with certainty whether our knowledge of them is valid or invalid'. Hammersley writes of this approach as 'subtle realism', arguing that it offers an alternative to the simple polarization between naïve forms of relativism and realism in modern discussions of ethnography.

The philosophy of social science literature of recent years offers him some support, at least in as much as defences of realism have proliferated. My own preference is for a development of the kinds of arguments advanced by Bhaskar (1979, 1987), who is not only concerned to establish a realist epistemology but also focuses upon ways of conceptualizing relations between social structure and agency. Broadly speaking, I would want to argue for an approach to research which recognizes that all methods for generating descriptive accounts (participant observation, ethnographic interview, questionnaires, historical narrative, statistical analysis, etc.) constitute starting points, individually and collectively, for explanatory analysis. That is to say, our goal should be to model social processes in such a way as to establish the mechanisms which underlie observed patterns. If, let us say, survey research into audiences suggests a finite set of response patterns in relation to particular television programming, then we would seek to show that the model that we have developed of audience activity in, say, a class context, provisionally makes sense of those patterns. We would then redescribe the situation in terms of the model and design further research (perhaps in-depth ethnographic interviews) that would allow us to examine and refine the theory. And so on, in a constant interaction of accounts generated by diverse methodologies with attempts to make theoretical sense of those accounts. There is no end to this process, of course, no final account, but through constant refinement, systematic comparison with alternative models and continuing reformulation we would seek to maximize 'ontological depth' – a richer, explanatory understanding of the patterns that characterize audience activity.

I am in agreement, then, with those who insist that we need empirically to examine the modes of audience activity. However, I do not consider that this purpose is best served by exclusive or even predominant use of 'ethnographic' methods. Some researchers clearly believe that audience ethnographies will provide privileged access to the inner workings of television viewing. This is simply not the case. What they can provide – in parallel with other methodological approaches – are accounts of patterned activity that provide grist for the explanatory mill. Such accounts, whatever the methodology used to generate them, are necessarily partial and can never simply be taken to represent participants' views. But nor are they nothing more than convenient fictions. Combined with research using other methodological approaches – triangulated, to borrow a jargon term – they potentially constitute an assembly of variously described materials in relation to which we formulate models. Clearly this returns theory to centre stage – it is within the terms of our theories that we develop models, and it is in relation to these models that we describe and redescribe the phenomenal world. But this is not 'Theory' in the grand capitalized sense. This is theory as a language of analysis and as an instrument of explanatory understanding.

It is through the development of this theory that the 'structural considerations' that Morley wants to incorporate into his ethnographic approach can be brought into play. But such theorizing cannot be an inductive by-product of audience ethnographies, as some researchers seem to assume. To construct models of audience activity we need to draw on theoretical as well as empirical resources, and, in particular, develop concepts which will allow for the conjoint conceptualization of structure and agency. I suggested earlier that cultural studies thinking has been restricted by a commitment to dualistic forms of theorizing, classically viewing structures as modes of ideological constraint, but more recently, in the rise of the active reader, affording considerable degrees of freedom to agents over structure. Audience ethnographies have swung with the theoretical pendulum toward the latter position, if not from theoretical intent, then as a matter of methodological default. This precisely parallels the kind of dualism that Giddens (1984) identifies as a basic difficulty in the development of modern sociological theories, and one which, he argues, can only be resolved by generating concepts which ensure that we understand structure and agency in conjoint terms – the one always implying and presupposing the other. This is the kind of thinking that will be essential in cultural studies if the newly emerged 'active reader' is to take her proper place.

Cultural populism

While the 'ethnographic' approach to incorporating active reader-ship into cultural studies is essentially methodological, vesting faith in empirical research into real readers, another possibility is to assert active readership as ontologically foundational and then reconstruct the cultural studies enterprise accordingly. A good example of this version of the swing away from strong ideology models, and one that has attracted a great deal of criticism and invective, is to be found in John Fiske's work, dubbed 'terminally uncritical populism' by McGuigan (1992: 49). Fiske and others are viewed as misbegotten products of the collapse of hegemony theory: 'under the strain of its own internal contradictions, the syn-thesis imploded and ultimately dissolved in the work of some authors, most notably John Fiske, into an uncritical celebration of mass-popular cultural consumption'. If we once lose sight of popu-lar culture's ideological function, the argument runs, and its embeddedness in specific political economies, then there is noth-ing left but to admire the capacity of creative readers in the diversity and inventiveness of their reading practices. What is wide-spread and popular is what is good, and no space remains for a critical cultural studies.

Of course, that is a caricature, and a very brief one at that, but it is not entirely unrepresentative of either 'uncritical cultural pop-ulism' or some of the attacks made upon it. What could provoke such division? Let us look more closely at Fiske's work in search of an answer. Just as the CCCS were, Fiske is concerned with culture in relation to resistance and power. As he formulates the issues in

Television Culture, however, and for all his willingness to invoke Vološinov as did the CCCS before him, his emphasis differs from that found in their account of hegemony and resistance. Drawing a key distinction between cultural and financial economies, he insists that the cultural economy has a degree of autonomy and 'that the power of audiences-as-producers in the cultural economy is considerable' (Fiske, 1987: 313). This is semiotic power, 'the power to construct meanings, pleasures, and social identities that *differ* from those proposed by the structures of domination' (*ibid*: 317). All this, of course, is not entirely at odds with the CCCS tradition, but as he begins to think through the implications of intertextuality, the difficulties encountered with the categories of 'text' and 'audience', the commodity character of television, and the whole postmodern turn (Fiske, 1989a, 1991) he begins increasingly to depart from orthodoxy.

These shifts lead to his 'attempt to outline a theory of popular culture in capitalist societies' (Fiske, 1989b: ix). Note the 'in capitalist societies'. If his position is indeed 'uncritical cultural populism' it is not one in which the capitalist social formation has entirely disappeared from the scene, even if it is not theorized as having quite the same ideological power as in earlier cultural studies theories. Historically, he suggests, popular culture had either been studied as an expression of collective social harmony or as an imposition of mass culture disempowering those caught within it. It is in a 'third direction' that Fiske's project is to move, and the passage in which he defines its distinctiveness is worth quoting in full.

> It, too, sees popular culture as a site of struggle, but, while accepting the power of the forces of dominance, it focuses rather upon the popular tactics by which these forces are coped with, are evaded or resisted. Instead of tracing exclusively the processes of incorporation, it investigates rather that popular vitality and creativity that

makes incorporation such a constant necessity. Instead of concentrating on the omnipresent, insidious practices of the dominant ideology, it attempts to understand the everyday resistances and evasions that make that ideology work so hard and insistently to maintain itself and its values. (*ibid*: 20–21)

The conceptual oppositions on which he is trading are clear enough here. On the one side: forces of dominance; processes of incorporation; insidious practices of the dominant ideology. On the other side: tactics for coping; vitality and creativity; everyday resistance and evasion. Dominance, incorporation and ideology are real enough in Fiske's account, then, but they are not central. Capitalist society is the locus of cultural contradictions and individual negotiations, and it is these processes that form the focus of Fiske's interest. The balance tips toward individuals, cultural tactics and micro-politics, and away from the macro-politics of hegemony theory.

In thus examining individual creativity and tactical resistance he draws primarily upon de Certeau (1984). The heart of the matter for Fiske lies in people's capacity to make their popular culture out of the materials that the system provides. But unlike views that concentrate on the ways in which the system thus limits people's activities and conceptions, Fiske prefers to accentuate the positive potential of this 'production in consumption'. 'All the culture industries can do,' he observes, 'is produce a repertoire of texts or cultural resources' (Fiske, 1989b: 24), as if that were trivial in comparison with the creative use to which such resources will then be put. His portrait is one of semiotic guerrilla warfare – a concept traceable back at least as far as Eco in an essay first published in 1967 (Eco, 1987) – in which people 'use guerrilla tactics against the strategies of the powerful, making poaching raids upon their texts or structures, and play constant tricks upon the system' (Fiske 1989b: 32). By 'reading' texts rather than merely 'deciphering' them – a distinction he borrows from de Certeau – popular cultural readers work against the system's language, a form of resistance promoting '*parole* over *langue*, practice over structure' (*ibid*: 108). Popular culture is thus the site of a struggle to use the system's cultural resources against the system itself, at least in the sense of opening up space for everyday resistance. Indeed, cultural resources only become *popular* culture because, for Fiske, the latter is by definition formed in a process of reacting against what he calls the 'forces of domination'.

Quite how these forces work is left largely unanalysed, presumably on the grounds that cultural studies has already paid more than enough attention to such issues. Yet periodically Fiske does retreat from the more extravagant rhetoric of cultural resistance. For example, in the course of discussing what he calls the 'producerly text' (a somewhat improbable conjunction of the accessibility of Barthes' 'readerly' text with the openness of his 'writerly' one) he concedes that a 'double focus' is required in analysing popular culture. The 'deep structures' of such texts show us domination in action, 'how insistently and insidiously the ideological forces of domination are at work in all the products of patriarchal consumer capitalism' (*ibid*: 105). But the pessimism that this insight engenders, where the only hope lies in radical revolution, must be counterbalanced by a more optimistic and 'complementary focus' on active cultural resistance. Traditional forms of analysis and criticism neglect this face of popular culture, he suggests, though one wonders where he might place CCCS work of the kind reported in *Resistance through Rituals* or all the appreciative criticism of popular genres scattered through the history of film studies. No doubt they remained too concerned to see popular forms as finally recuperated by the dominant ideology.

There is, then, a frustrating tendency in Fiske's account to reach for the rhetoric of semiotic resistance whenever more structural

considerations sneak to the fore. Clearly he sees himself correcting
an imbalance, and there are indeed conceptual imbalances in need
of correction in cultural studies. Whether Fiske's somewhat
romantic optimism about the potential for resistance in popular
culture is the appropriate theoretical strategy, however, is not so
clear. That optimism, and the celebratory tone that attends it,
surely leads to equally problematic imbalances in the other direction. Consider, for example, his repeated insistence that popular
culture is 'progressive'. 'Popular culture always has a progressive
potential,' he says (*ibid*: 177), by which he means that the materials
of popular culture can be and are utilized to construct resistance in
the micro-politics of everyday life. 'Its progressiveness is concerned with redistributing power within these structures [family,
work, classroom] toward the disempowered; it attempts to enlarge
the space within which bottom-up power has to operate' (*ibid*: 56).
Sometimes he seems to write as if this potential was always
realised in the very existence of popular culture, a claim which is
trivially true in that, for Fiske, *real* popular culture is definitionally
made by consumers in the act of resistance. But (popular) cultural
resources are surely used just as often at the micro-political level in
sustaining existing power relations, and constantly to stress their
progressive use is to lose sight of the complexity of micro-politics
in the cause of an overstated corrective to the 'pessimistic reductionism' (*ibid*: 192) of incorporation arguments. Although it is true
that people use culture of all kinds to resist the constraints of
everyday life, that is by no means its only or even its dominant use.

Does this work represent an uncritical populist drift in cultural
studies, as McGuigan (1992: 171–172) suggests, founded on an
'increasingly sentimental' solidarity with ordinary people and over-
attention to micro-processes of meaning construction? In general
terms we have to concede that it probably does, although Fiske's
tendency periodically to qualify and even contradict his stronger

claims does mean that it is possible to construct readings of his position that are less open to McGuigan's swingeing criticisms. One such reading and defence is that of Storey (1993: 182–199), who rightly observes that McGuigan's and others' assertion of the superiority of an alternative political economy approach to culture is not self-evident. I shall not follow this argument through here, not because it is unimportant, but because it falls into precisely the dualistic traps that mar cultural populism in the first place. If it was the perceived one-sidedness of traditional top-down views that gave rise to Fiske's and others' excess of bottom-up rhetoric, then to respond to the latter in the same terms is a recipe for endless and futile oscillation between opposed positions.

The more interesting question to ask is, do the cultural populist attempts to rewrite the cultural studies project in the light of an ontology of active readership resolve the problems that occasioned their emergence in the first place? The answer to this question is surely no, for the simple reason that they remain trapped within the same dualistic framework as those against whom they react. What is required is not an insistence on micro-meanings and cre-ativity *against* macro-structures and constraint, but an attempt to rethink the form of relation between these two in non-reductive and non-dualistic terms. In examining this possibility in the context of social theory, Giddens suggests that a general distinction between what he calls 'objectivism' and 'subjectivism' lies behind such dualistic conceptions. 'By the former of these notions,' he writes (Giddens, 1986: 530), 'I mean that perspective in social theory according to which the social object – that is society – has priority over the individual agent, and in which social institutions are regarded as the core component of interest to social analysis. Subjectivism essentially means its opposite. According to this standpoint, the human agent is treated as the prime center for social analysis.' The drift toward subjectivism that Giddens saw in

1970s sociology is exactly paralleled in modern cultural studies, bringing with it all the familiar conceptual and methodological difficulties born of an unreflective dualism of structure and agency.

Paradigm lost?

Is there, then, a 'paradigm crisis' in cultural studies? Certainly there are those who would suggest as much on the basis of exactly those reader-centred developments that we have been considering in this chapter. On this account, cultural studies (and media studies too, for the 'crisis' is also seen there) was making some progress in its neo-Gramscian form, if, perhaps, still too text oriented. However, the spread of subjectivism in the form of audience ethnography and cultural populism has undermined such progress, and their claims to innovative thinking are no more than old ideas given new currency. As a result, the project of a distinctively critical cultural studies has been set back.

Curran's (1990) attack on what he calls the 'new revisionist movement' in media and cultural studies is a good instance of this kind of argument. To appreciate how the case is made it is necessary to have some idea of the recent history of media research as Curran views it. According to him, the 1970s saw the development of critical alternatives to the prevailing pluralist views of the role of the media in society. One of those alternatives – that in which Curran himself was closely involved – adopted a political economy framework and was concerned especially with ownership of the media and the relation of that to the workings of the state. The other was broadly that associated with the CCCS in the heyday of its focus upon ideology and hegemony. Although these two schools of thought differed in many ways, they coincided in their commitment to a broadly marxist analysis of the media and thus constituted something of a radical critical development in media research. During the 1980s, however, revision became necessary, above all because of 'growing disenchantment with the class conflict model of society that framed much of its [the radical tradition's] research output' (Curran, 1990: 139).

This revision took various forms (including compromises between radical and pluralist traditions in media studies) but was particularly far-reaching, in Curran's view, in the prominent and growing concern with audience reception. 'This is an area of media research that has been extensively mythologized,' he observes acidly (*ibid*: 145), going on to suggest that the belief that 'new' audience analysis is excitingly innovative is only possible in the context of a foreshortened misreading of the history of communications research. There are plenty of precursors to reception studies, he claims, not least the long-established 'uses and gratifications' model. The new revisionism is therefore engaged in 'rediscovering the wheel', which would not matter were it not for the loss of critical edge that this entails. All too often it has 'resulted in old pluralist dishes being reheated and presented as new cuisine' (*ibid*: 151).

Of course, Curran is being somewhat disingenuous here. Although 'new revisionism' does indeed turn attention away from a direct concern with the structuring impact on the media of politico-economic factors, it cannot straightforwardly be equated with the pluralist and functionalist analyses espoused in uses and gratifications research. As Ang (1996: 42) observes in drawing this very distinction, unlike the uses and gratifications project the aim of new audience research 'is to arrive at a more historicized and contextualized insight into the ways in which "audience activity" is articulated within and by a complex set of social, political, economic and cultural forces'. In the present theoretical circumstances this may be something of a utopian aim, but it is certainly true that the emergence of new revisionism in a specifically cultural studies context does make it a distinctly different beast to superficially similar revisions of the orthodox mass communications tradition. Nevertheless, as we have seen earlier in this chapter's discussion, there is some force to the claim that new revisionism is significantly less critical than its predecessors, not because it is doing no more than repeat previous errors in new guises, but because in embracing subjectivism it finds its focus restricted in empirical, theoretical and evaluative terms.

In response to that, there is a tendency in critiques of new revisionism to suppose that reincorporating political economy considerations will return cultural studies to its proper critical role. McGuigan (1992: 160), for instance, in resisting what he calls the 'essentially hermeneutic perspective' of the likes of Ang and Morley, argues that macro-dynamics cannot be understood satisfactorily where 'interpretation of cultural consumption [is] always firmly at the centre of the analytic picture'. These 'complex and obscure dynamics', he continues, 'are fundamentally about the disposition of material resources, corporate decision-making and capital investment'. While much of my discussion in this chapter would reinforce the first part of his claim – that making audience interpretation the analytic focus is not conducive to extending our grasp of macro-dynamics – it is surely not the case that such dynamics are 'fundamentally' of the material and economic form that he then proposes. Certainly the apparatus of global capitalism is significant in understanding macro-processes at work in modern media; but so too is a variety of other, non-economic features of the ways in which our social lives are systematically structured. If the critical cultural studies paradigm has indeed been lost, return to a version of the reductionism that flawed it in the first place is not an ideal strategy to bring about its resurrection. As a disconsolate Curran (1990: 158) himself observes at the end of his discussion, there has been a sea-change that 'will reshape – for better or worse – the development of media and cultural studies in Europe'. Paradigm lost, then, is unlikely to be followed by paradigm regained.

It may, however, be followed by 'paradigm changed' in as much as there is a welcome inclination in modern cultural studies to explore alternatives to both the older 'objectivist' traditions and the current 'subjectivist' candidates to replace them. Murdock (1989: 227), for example, invokes Bourdieu, Giddens and philosophical realism in arguing for a project that 'must move beyond immediate acts of consumption and response to analyze the underlying structures that provide the contexts and resources for audience activity and go on to demonstrate how they organize the making and taking of meaning in everyday life'. This requires a more positive response to the 'paradigm crisis' than that involved in reasserting the primacy of previously established positions, though it may – indeed, it should – draw upon those earlier traditions in pursuit of a new synthesis. At various points in this chapter I have suggested certain of the questions that I think such an attempt should address. Here I want to pull some of those threads together in an avowedly schematic account of the main parameters of the 'crisis' in cultural studies.

To the extent that there really is a paradigm crisis – and leaving aside any difficulties that arise from the increasing diffuseness of the very term 'cultural studies' – division and confusion seem to me to operate along four main dimensions. One is largely theoretical, though its consequences are more ramified, revolving around differences in conceptualizing the most fundamental ontological features of culture and social life. This is the area on which I have touched most frequently in this book, generally in the form of the 'structure-agency problem'. The second dimension is methodological and epistemological, posing questions about the kinds of knowledge that cultural studies seeks and about the methodologies best suited to the task of establishing such knowledge. The third is primarily political, involving differences about the critical positions that cultural studies should or could adopt in analysing the role of cultural forms in modern societies. And the fourth raises related questions of aesthetics and evaluation, asking whether and in what degree cultural studies should seek to make judgements of quality about the artefacts that it examines. Needless to say, all four interrelate in a variety of ways. Linked issues of theory, method, politics and aesthetics have featured prominently in the short lifetime of cultural studies, so it is hardly surprising to find that they form the main fault-lines along which divisions open up in times of change.

I shall consider these four dimensions in reverse order, beginning with what some might argue is the most long-lived but least interesting issue: the problem of making judgements of quality. In cultural studies' earliest manifestations the question of quality was clearly to the fore. Exponents of the culture and civilization tradition saw discrimination between 'good' and 'bad' culture as central to the whole enterprise, as did their revisionist successors such as Hoggart, Williams, and those who sought to demonstrate that popular culture, too, was capable of profundity and seriousness of purpose. This much we saw in Chapter 2. The arrival of structuralism, however, signalled a move away from issues of quality, encouraging questions about how it was that cultural artefacts actually functioned rather than seeking to make judgements about their aesthetic and moral value. This is not to suggest that evaluative concerns disappeared entirely. There has always remained at least a residual interest in critical discrimination, a topic given periodic renewal in highly publicized attempts to define the 'canon' in different cultural forms – especially literature – or to rescue commonly devalued texts (such as soap opera) through a strategy of redemptive reading (cf. Brunsdon, 1991).

For all the attention attracted by such endeavours, however, post-structuralist cultural studies has not generally focused on discrimination as an end in itself. The presumption that it was possible and desirable to categorize both individual artefacts and whole cultural forms in terms of fixed standards of quality had fallen into some disrepute long before the 'postmodern' fashion for aesthetic and moral relativism. In practice, aesthetic discrimination had been absorbed into more all-encompassing judgements about the social and political role played by particular forms and texts. And while there is sometimes an element of cultural evaluation in the allegations of 'uncritical cultural populism' directed at recent reader-oriented cultural studies – especially in attributing to the likes of Fiske a 'what is popular is what is good' position – the more forceful arguments have tended to bemoan the loss of a critical edge in political rather than aesthetic terms. It has certainly been argued that recent cultural studies has forgone the capacity to make critical statements about the texts on which it focuses, its emphasis on active readers permitting only the articulation of different readers' diverse points of view. But the alternative vantage point proposed by such challenges is based not so much in the domain of aesthetics as in that of politics.

To be 'critical' then, in the terms posed by those unhappy with recent cultural studies, is to relocate texts and readers back into the socio-political context from which, allegedly, they have been removed. Judgements of quality now become judgements about the ideological role of texts and their social consequences, informed by a political economy of the media and a more general account of the operation of capitalist social formations. In this argument, the uncritical pluralism of audience-centred perspectives is contrasted with what is presumed to be a more desirable critical holism. Note, however, that there are two analytically separate issues here: one depends upon making a general case in favour of holism; the other seeks to use holistic understanding of the socio-political role of cultural forms as a basis for critical assessment.

On the first issue it is difficult not to feel some sympathy with the critics of audience-oriented studies. Though the rise of the reader has not necessarily precluded a fully contextual account of readership – indeed, that has been the stated goal of such researchers as Ang and Morley – the net result has been the proliferation of detailed micro-studies at the expense of macro-understanding. Lacking the theoretical and methodological resources necessary to make the micro–macro connections, recent cultural studies has all too often defaulted into forms of 'ethnographic' description from which structural considerations are largely absent. On the second issue, things are less straightforward. Whilst I have no inclination to bemoan the lack of a post-Leavisite critical sensibility in modern cultural studies, it is at least arguable that making informed judgements about cultural materials in terms of their socio-political significance is a necessary part of any adequate analysis of culture. To that degree, cultural studies should indeed be 'critical'. What is not so clear is whether the kinds of theoretical alternatives posed by critics of 'cultural populism' or 'the new revisionism' would do the required job. They may be right to draw attention to the drift toward pluralism in cultural studies theory, but this does not mean that superseded neo-Gramscian models should be returned to centre stage. Some form of critical holism may well be necessary, but it must be a holism that can grapple with precisely those previously unaddressed concerns that have occasioned the turn toward audience-oriented work: pleasure, processes of readership, polysemy, and the manipulative use of popular culture by social agents.

Whatever one's position on the aesthetic and political

dimensions of the 'crisis', discussion quickly leads back to broader theoretical and methodological issues. And even if all aspirations to make critical judgements are dismissed, whether aesthetic or socio-political, there still remains a substantial core of method-ological and theoretical difficulties. Consider methodology. As we saw in the first section of this chapter, although methodological self-consciousness has not loomed large in the cultural studies lit-erature, where it has recently come to the fore it has been more concerned with the 'problem' of the partiality of ethnographic infor-mation than with more general issues of epistemology and method. Furthermore, while it is true that a division between methodolog-ical individualism and methodological holism is implicit in several of the critiques of 'cultural populism', there has not been any sus-tained discussion of such issues. Now this is hardly the place to re-examine either the lengthy debate about methodological indi-vidualism in the social sciences (cf. O'Neill, 1973) or those more general epistemological arguments that emerged as a result of sociology's 1970s move toward more ethnographically inclined methodologies. While cultural studies may well have something to learn from the earlier methodological travails of its sister social science disciplines, it can only do so by exploring those method-ological problems as they are now encountered in a cultural studies context.

In these circumstances, furthermore, the logically prior episte-mological issue – the problem that underlies specific divisions already touched on in this chapter, such as individualism versus holism or ethnographic description versus structural explanation – is the lack of clarity in cultural studies about the status and function of 'theory'. For some, theory has meant no more than generaliza-tion – statements that go beyond specific textual descriptions or evaluations. For others, theory equates to philosophy at least in as much as the latter is understood to involve speculative and abstract contemplation of matters cultural. Yet others have seen the theorizing process as central to the very constitution of 'reality' itself, or, not unconnected, as part of the process of 'deconstructing' the worlds constituted in culture. Others invoke 'theory' to decode texts, to unpack ideologies, to lend legitimacy and apparent coherence to judgements of value or moral worth. In the short history of cultural studies, the term has been employed to designate a multitude of abstractions, generalizations and speculations. Yet rarely has anyone stopped to consider the purpose of all this theorizing or what relation it might bear to the kind of knowledge that we seek. In consequence, those occupying different positions have all too often talked past each other – witness some of the 'debates' in the recent literature – leaning upon quite different epistemologies in promoting their cases. An outside observer, however benevolently disposed, would find it well nigh impossible to identify any common epistemological foundation on which the cultural studies project is built.

I have outlined my own position earlier in this chapter, preferring an instrumental concept of theory located within a broadly realist epistemology. From this point of view, the aim of cultural studies is explanatory understanding of the realm of culture: texts, readers, and the relation of both to their larger social context. By building abstract (and inevitably simplified) models of these processes, we seek to make sense of observed patterns of human activity, observations that are made, of course, using methodological devices which are themselves theoretically grounded. Provided that the theories on which observations depend are not the same as the theories invoked for explanation, circularity can be avoided, and provided that the methodologies applied are sufficiently diverse, the risk of methodological monism is minimized. In this way, the models or 'theories' that we generate can be assessed against each other as instruments of explanation.

But even if this kind of realism is unacceptable – and I have not tried to make a sustained case for it here – the problems to which it is a response are real enough. Whatever the preferred solution, what has to be avoided is a situation in which theories become all but immune to empirical arbitration, and research methodologies – where they are considered at all – are cast in terms of one acceptable route to truth. This is the situation that has characterized cultural studies for much of its history, and which continues to do so in its time of 'crisis'. Only by systematic epistemological reflection and debate can we hope to overcome such widespread methodological confusion.

Lurking behind these epistemological issues we find still more basic theoretical divisions, above all those reflecting fundamental assumptions about the nature of social and cultural reality. In the course of this book I have tried to show the ways in which 'top-down' accounts of the relationship between people and their culture have dominated cultural studies thinking, whether in the form of subject-positioning theories or dominant ideology models. Although there are undoubted differences between the perspectives here represented by *Screen* theory and the work of the CCCS, on this matter – and for all the CCCS' insistence on its interest in active agency – they broadly coincide. In Giddens' sense quoted earlier, they are 'objectivist' in inclination, viewing society (via culture and ideology) as having priority over the individual. We have seen how these traditions of thought faced increasing difficulties in conceptualizing various features of culture that simply would not fit into predominantly top-down forms of analysis. These failings bred dissatisfaction, and from that dissatisfaction has come an accelerating drift toward more 'bottom-up' perspectives in the shape of, among others, audience ethnography and 'cultural populism'.

What we see in audience ethnography and cultural populism is a determined attempt to move cultural studies toward subjectivism, the one in terms of its methodological strategy, the other in its basic commitment to the primacy of the agent. In principle, of course, exponents of both positions recognize the need to incorporate structural considerations. In practice, however, they do no such thing, caught as they are by the methodological individualism of 'thick description' or the over-active agent of theoretical subjectivism. 'Members of elaborated societies,' Fiske (1989a: 181) suggests, 'are social agents rather than social subjects.' But the point of distinguishing social agency and social structure is precisely to understand how it is that people are *both* social subjects *and* social agents. We exist as social beings in consequence of pre-existing social practices that are experienced by us, via culture, as structured. And it is the very presence of such structures that makes us social agents; without them we would not have access to the materials necessary for us to produce and reproduce our social activities. Without structures, then, there can be no social agents; without social agents, there is no structure. Any approach that attends to one at the expense of the other – whether by methodological default or theoretical fiat – is simply failing to recognize that they are profoundly implicated in each other, and that both our methodologies and our theories need to recognize that. Without theories and methods that will allow us to inquire into this dialectic of structure and agency, we shall be doomed continually to tumble into the delusions of subjectivism or objectivism. It is the resolution of this dilemma that is the most urgent task facing us today. If it cannot be resolved, then there is indeed a real crisis in cultural studies.

References

Abercrombie, N. (1990) 'Popular Culture and Ideological Effects', pp. 199–228 in N. Abercrombie, S. Hill and B. S. Turner (eds) *Dominant Ideologies*. London: Unwin Hyman.

Abercrombie, N., Hill, S., and Turner, B. S. (eds) (1980) *The Dominant Ideology Thesis*. London: George Allen & Unwin.

Althusser, L. (1969) *For Marx*. Harmondsworth: Penguin Books.

Althusser, L. (1977) *Lenin and Philosophy and Other Essays*. London: NLB.

Anderson, P. (1968) 'Components of the National Culture', *New Left Review*, 50: 3–57.

Ang, I. (1985) *Watching Dallas: Soap Opera and the Melodramatic Imagination*. London and New York: Methuen.

Ang, I. (1996) *Living Room Wars: Rethinking Media Audiences for a Postmodern World*. London and New York: Routledge.

Arnold, M. ([1869] 1960) *Culture and Anarchy*. London: Cambridge University Press.

Barthes, R. (1973) *Elements of Semiology*. New York: Hill & Wang.

Barthes, R. (1977a) *Image – Music – Text*. London: Fontana/Collins.

Barthes, R. (1977b) 'Introduction to the Structural Analysis of Narratives', pp. 79–124 in R. Barthes, *Image – Music – Text*. London: Fontana/Collins.

Barthes, R. (1977c) 'The Photographic Message', pp. 15–31 in R. Barthes, *Image – Music – Text*. London: Fontana/Collins.

Barthes, R. (1983) *The Fashion System*. New York: Hill & Wang.

Barthes, R. (1990) *S/Z*. Oxford: Basil Blackwell.

Barthes, R. (1993) *Mythologies*. London: Vintage Books.

Berelson, B. (1952) *Content Analysis in Communication Research*. Glencoe, IL: Free Press.

Bhaskar, R. (1979) *The Possibility of Naturalism*. Brighton: Harvester Press.

Bhaskar, R. (1987) *Scientific Realism and Human Emancipation*. London: Verso.

Bineham, J. L. (1988) 'A Historical Account of the Hypodermic Model in Mass Communication', *Communication Monographs* 55: 230–246.

Bourdieu, P. (1977) *Outline of a Theory of Practice*. Cambridge: Cambridge University Press.

Bourdieu, P. (1986) *Distinction: A Social Critique of the Judgement of Taste*. London: Routledge.

Brunsdon, C. (1991) 'Text and Audience', pp. 116–129 in E. Seiter, H. Borchers, G. Kreutzner, and E-M. Warth (eds) *Remote Control: Television, Audiences, and Cultural Power*. London and New York: Routledge.

Brunsdon, C. and Morley, D. (1978) *Everyday Television: 'Nationwide'*. London: British Film Institute.

Buckingham, D. (1987) *Public Secrets: 'Eastenders' and its Audience*. London: British Film Institute.

Buscombe, E., Gledhill, C., Lovell, A. and Williams, C. (1975/76) 'Statement: Psychoanalysis and Film', *Screen*, 16, 4: 119–130.

Buscombe, E., Gledhill, C., Lovell, A. and Williams, C. (1976) 'Statement: Why We Have Resigned from the Board of *Screen*', *Screen*, 17, 2: 106–109.

Carey, J. W. (1989) *Communication as Culture: Essays on Media and Society*. Boston: Unwin Hyman.

Carey, J. W. and Kreiling, A. L. (1974) 'Popular Culture and Uses and Gratifications: Notes toward an Accommodation', pp. 225–248 in J. G. Blumler and E. Katz (eds) *The Uses of Mass Communications: Current Perspectives on Gratifications Research*. Beverly Hills and London: Sage Publications.

Centre for Contemporary Cultural Studies (1978) *On Ideology*. London: Hutchinson.

Centre for Contemporary Cultural Studies (1982) *The Empire Strikes Back: Race and Racism in 70s Britain*. London: Hutchinson.

Centre for Contemporary Cultural Studies, Women's Studies Group (1978) *Women Take Issue: Aspects of Women's Subordination*. London: Hutchinson.

Chaney, D. (1994) *The Cultural Turn: Scene-Setting Essays on Contemporary Cultural History*. London and New York: Routledge.

Chodorow, N. (1978) *The Reproduction of Mothering: Psychoanalysis and the Sociology of Gender*. Berkeley: University of California Press.

Clarke, J., Hall, S., Jefferson, T. and Roberts, B. (1976) 'Subcultures, Cultures and Class: a Theoretical Overview', pp. 9–74 in S. Hall and T. Jefferson (eds) *Resistance through Rituals: Youth Subcultures in Post-war Britain*. London: Hutchinson.

Clarke, J., Critcher, C. and Johnson, R. (eds) (1979) *Working Class Culture: Studies in History and Theory*. London: Hutchinson.

Clifford, C. and Marcus, G. E. (eds) (1986) *Writing Culture: The Poetics and Politics of Ethnography*. Berkeley, Los Angeles and London: University of California Press.

Coward, R. (1977) 'Class, "Culture" and the Social Formation', *Screen*, 18, 1: 75–105.

Coward, R. and Ellis, J. (1977) *Language and Materialism: Developments in Semiology and the Theory of the Subject*. London: Routledge & Kegan Paul.

Culler, J. (1975) *Structuralist Poetics*. London: Routledge & Kegan Paul.

Culler, J. (1986) *Saussure*. London: Fontana.

Culler, J. (1990) *Barthes*. London: Fontana.

Curran, J. (1990) 'The New Revisionism in Mass Communication Research: a Reappraisal', *European Journal of Communication*, 5: 135–164.

de Certeau, M. (1984) *The Practice of Everyday Life*. Berkeley: University of California Press.

Dyer, R., Geraghty, C., Jordan, M., Lovell, T., Paterson, R. and Stewart, J. (1981) *Coronation Street*. London: British Film Institute.

Eco, U. (1987) 'Towards a Semiological Guerrilla Warfare', pp. 135–144 in U. Eco, *Travels in Hyper-Reality*. London: Picador.

Editors of *Cahiers du Cinéma* (1972) 'John Ford's *Young Mr Lincoln*', *Screen*, 13, 3: 5–44.

Ellis, J. (1977) 'Introduction' in *Screen Reader 1: Cinema/Ideology/Politics*. London: Society for Education in Film and Television.

Fiske, J. (1987) *Television Culture*. London: Methuen.

Fiske, J. (1989a) 'Moment of Television: Neither the Text nor the Audience', pp. 56–78 in E. Seiter, H. Borchers, G. Kreutzner and E-M. Warth (eds) *Remote Control: Television, Audiences, and Cultural Power*. London and New York: Routledge.

Fiske, J. (1989b) *Understanding Popular Culture*. London and New York: Routledge.

Fiske, J. (1991) 'Postmodernism and Television', pp. 55–67 in J. Curran and M. Gurevitch (eds) *Mass Media and Society*. London: Edward Arnold.

Franklin, S., Lury, C. and Stacey, J. (eds) (1991) *Off Centre: Feminism and Cultural Studies*. London: HarperCollins.

Frow, J. (1995) *Cultural Studies and Cultural Value*. Oxford: Clarendon Press.

Gamman, L. (1988) 'Watching the Detectives: the Enigma of the Female Gaze', pp. 8–26 in L. Gamman and M. Marshment (eds) *The Female Gaze: Women as Viewers of Popular Culture*. London: The Women's Press.

Gamman, L. and Marshment, M. (eds) (1988) *The Female Gaze: Women as Viewers of Popular Culture*. London: The Women's Press.

Garfinkel, H. (1967) *Studies in Ethnomethodology*. Englewood Cliffs, NJ: Prentice-Hall.

Geertz, C. (1973) *The Interpretation of Cultures*. New York: Basic Books.

Geraghty, C. (1991) *Women and Soap Opera: A Study of Prime Time Soaps*. Cambridge: Polity Press.

Gerbner, G. and Gross, L. (1976) 'Living with Television: the Violence Profile', *Journal of Communication*, 26, 2: 173–199.

Gerbner, G., Holsti, O. R., Krippendorf, K., Paisley, W. J. and Stone, P. J. (eds) (1969) *The Analysis of Communication Content*. New York, London, Sydney and Toronto: John Wiley & Sons.

Gerbner, G., Gross, L., Morgan, M. and Signorielli, N. (1986) 'Living with Television: the Dynamics of the Cultivation Process', pp. 17–40 in J. Bryant and D. Zillmann (eds) *Perspectives on Media Effects*. Hillsdale, NJ and London: Lawrence Erlbaum Associates.

Giddens, A. (1984) *The Constitution of Society: Outline of the Theory of Structuration*. Cambridge: Polity Press.

Giddens, A. (1986) 'Action, Subjectivity, and the Constitution of Meaning', *Social Research*, 53: 529–545.

Gray, A. (1992) *Video Playtime: the Gendering of a Leisure Technology*. London: Routledge.

Hall, S. (1978) 'The Hinterland of Science: Ideology and the "Sociology of Knowledge"', pp. 9–32 in CCCS, *On Ideology*. London: Hutchinson.

Hall, S. (1980a) 'Cultural Studies and the Centre: Some Problematics and Problems', pp. 15–47 in S. Hall, D. Hobson, A. Lowe and P. Willis (eds) *Culture, Media, Language*. London: Hutchinson.

Hall, S. (1980b) 'Cultural Studies: Two Paradigms', *Media, Culture and Society*, 2: 57–72.

Hall, S. (1980c) 'Recent Developments in Theories of Language and Ideology: a Critical Note', pp. 157–162 in S. Hall, D. Hobson, A. Lowe and P. Willis (eds) *Culture, Media, Language*. London: Hutchinson.

Hall, S. (1980d) 'Encoding/Decoding', pp. 128–138 in S. Hall, D. Hobson, A. Lowe and P. Willis (eds) *Culture, Media, Language*. London: Hutchinson.

Hall, S. (1982) 'The Rediscovery of "Ideology": Return of the Repressed in Media Studies', pp. 56–90 in M. Gurevitch, T. Bennett, J. Curran and J. Woollacott (eds) *Culture, Society and the Media*. London: Routledge.

Hall, S. (1996) 'The Problem of Ideology: Marxism without Guarantees', pp. 25–46 in D. Morley and K-H. Chen (eds) *Stuart Hall: Critical Dialogues in Cultural Studies*. London: Routledge.

Hall, S. (1997) 'The Television Discourse – Encoding and Decoding', pp. 28–34 in A. Gray and J. McGuigan (eds) *Studying Culture: An Introductory Reader*. Second Edition. London: Arnold.

Hall, S. and Jefferson, T. (eds) (1976) *Resistance through Rituals: Youth Subcultures in Post-war Britain*. London: Hutchinson.

Hall, S. and Whannel, P. (1964) *The Popular Arts*. London: Hutchinson Educational.

Hall, S., Lumley, B. and McLennan, G. (1978) 'Politics and Ideology: Gramsci', pp. 45–76 in CCCS, *On Ideology*. London: Hutchinson.

Hall, S., Hobson, D., Lowe, A. and Willis, P. (eds) (1980) *Culture, Media, Language*. London: Hutchinson.

Hammersley, M. (1992) *What's Wrong with Ethnography?* London: Routledge.

Heath, S. (1973) 'The Work of Christian Metz', *Screen*, 14, 3: 5–28.

Hebdige, D. (1979) *Subculture: The Meaning of Style*. London: Methuen.

Hindess, B. and Hirst, P. (1977) *Modes of Production and Social Formation: An Auto-Critique of 'Pre-Capitalist Modes of Production'*. London: Macmillan.

Hobson, D. (1982) *Crossroads: the Drama of a Soap Opera*. London: Methuen.

Hoggart, R. ([1957] 1958) *The Uses of Literacy*. Harmondsworth: Penguin Books.

Holsti, O. R. (1969) *Content Analysis for the Social Sciences and Humanities*. Reading, MA: Addison-Wesley.

James, A., Hockey, J. and Dawson, A. (eds) (1997) *After Writing Culture: Epistemology and Praxis in Contemporary Anthropology*. London and New York: Routledge.

Jancovich, M. (1995) 'Screen Theory', pp. 123–150 in J. Hollows and M. Jancovich (eds) *Approaches to Popular Film*. Manchester and New York: Manchester University Press.

Johnson, R. (1986) 'What is Cultural Studies Anyway?' *Social Text*, 16: 38–80.

Katz, E. and Lazarsfeld, P. F. (1955) *Personal Influence: The Part Played by People in the Flow of Mass Communciation*. Glencoe, IL: Free Press.

Klapper, J. T. (1960) *The Effects of Mass Communication*. New York: Free Press.

Klapper, J. T. (1963) 'Mass Communication Research: an Old Road Resurveyed', *Public Opinion Quarterly*, 27: 515–527.

Kuhn, A. (1984) 'Women's Genres', *Screen*, 25, 1: 18–28.

Kurzweil, E. (1980) *The Age of Structuralism: Lévi-Strauss to Foucault*. New York: Columbia University Press.

Lacan, J. (1977) *Écrits: A Selection*. London: Tavistock.

Lapsley, R. and Westlake, M. (1988) *Film Theory: An Introduction*. Manchester: Manchester University Press.

Leach, E. (1970) *Lévi-Strauss*. London: Fontana/Collins.

Leavis, F. R. (1930) *Mass Civilisation and Minority Culture*. Cambridge: The Minority Press.

Leavis, F. R. (1952) *The Common Pursuit*. London: Chatto & Windus.

Leavis, F. R. (1960) *The Great Tradition: George Eliot, Henry James, Joseph Conrad*. London: Chatto & Windus.

Leavis, F. R. and Thompson, D. (1933) *Culture and Environment: The Training of Critical Awareness*. London: Chatto & Windus.

Leavis, Q. D. (1932) *Fiction and the Reading Public*. London: Chatto & Windus.

Lévi-Strauss, C. (1970) *The Raw and the Cooked*. London: Jonathan Cape.

Lévi-Strauss, C. (1972) *Structural Anthropology*. Harmondsworth: Penguin Books.

Lévi-Strauss, C. (1973) *From Honey to Ashes*. London: Jonathan Cape.

Lévi-Strauss, C. (1978) *The Origin of Table Manners*. London: Jonathan Cape.

Lévi-Strauss, C. (1990) *The Naked Man*. London: Jonathan Cape.

Lovell, A. (1969) 'Robin Wood – a Dissenting View', *Screen*, 10, 2: 42–55.

Lovell, T. (1980) *Pictures of Reality: Aesthetics, Politics, Pleasure*. London: BFI Publishing.

Lovell, T. (1981) 'Ideology and *Coronation Street*', pp. 40–52 in R. Dyer, C. Geraghty, M. Jordan, T. Lovell, R. Paterson and J. Stewart, *Coronation Street*. London: British Film Institute.

Lovell, T. (ed.) (1995) *Feminist Cultural Studies (Volumes I and II)*. Aldershot and Brookfield, VT: Edward Elgar.

Lull, J. (1980) 'The Social Uses of Television', *Human Communication Research*, 6, 3: 197–209.

MacCabe, C. (1974) 'Realism and the Cinema: Notes on some Brechtian Theses', *Screen*, 15, 2: 7–27.

Mayne, J. (1993) *Cinema and Spectatorship*. London: Routledge.

McGuigan, J. (1992) *Cultural Populism*. London and New York: Routledge.

McRobbie, A. (1978) 'Working Class Girls and the Culture of Femininity', pp. 96–108 in Centre for Contemporary Cultural Studies, Women's Studies Group, *Women Take Issue: Aspects of Women's Subordination*. London: Hutchinson.

McRobbie, A. (1991a) *Feminism and Youth Culture: From 'Jackie' to 'Just Seventeen'*. London: Macmillan.

McRobbie, A. (1991b) 'New Times in Cultural Studies', *New Formations*, 13: 1–17.

Metz, C. (1974a) *Film Language: A Semiotics of the Cinema*. New York: Oxford University Press.

Metz, C. (1974b) *Language and Cinema*. The Hague: Mouton.

Metz, C. (1975) 'The Imaginary Signifier', *Screen*, 16, 2: 14–76.

Metz, C. (1982) *Psychoanalysis and Cinema: The Imaginary Signifier*. London: Macmillan.

Mills, C. W. (1959) *The Power Elite*. New York: Oxford University Press.

Mitchell, J. (1974) *Psychoanalysis and Feminism*. Harmondsworth: Penguin Books.

Modleski, T. (1982) *Loving with a Vengeance: Mass Produced Fantasies for Women*. London and New York: Methuen.

Moores, S. (1993) *Interpreting Audiences: The Ethnography of Media Consumption*. London: Sage Publications.

Morley, D. (1980a) 'Texts, Readers, Subjects', pp. 163–173 in S. Hall, D. Hobson, A. Lowe and P. Willis (eds) *Culture, Media, Language*. London: Hutchinson.

Morley, D. (1980b) *The 'Nationwide' Audience*. London: British Film Institute.

Morley, D. (1981) '*The "Nationwide" Audience*: a Critical Postscript', *Screen Education*, 39: 3–14.

Morley, D. (1986) *Family Television*. London: Routledge.

Morley, D. (1992) *Television, Audiences and Cultural Studies*. London: Routledge.

Mulhern, F. (1979) *The Moment of 'Scrutiny'*. London: New Left Books.

Mulvey, L. (1975) 'Visual Pleasure and Narrative Cinema', *Screen*, 16, 3: 6–18.

Mulvey, L. (1989) 'British Feminist Film Theory's Female Spectators: Presence and Absence', *Camera Obscura*, 20/21: 68–81.

Mulvey, L. (1990) 'Afterthoughts on "Visual Pleasure and Narrative Cinema" inspired by *Duel in the Sun*', pp. 24–35 in E. A. Kaplan (ed.) *Psychoanalysis & Cinema*. London and New York: Routledge.

Murdock, G. (1989) 'Critical Inquiry and Audience Activity', pp. 226–249 in B. Dervin, L. Grossberg, B. J. O'Keefe and E. Wartella (eds) *Rethinking Communication. Volume 2 Paradigm Exemplars*. London: Sage Publications.

North, R. C., Holsti, O. R., Zaninovich, M. G. and Zinnes, D. A. (1963) *Content Analysis: A Handbook with Applications for the Study of International Crisis*. Evanston, IL: Northwestern University.

O'Neill, J. (ed.) (1973) *Modes of Individualism and Collectivism*. London: Heinemann.

Pawson, R. (1989) *A Measure for Measures*. London and New York: Routledge.

Pool, I. de Sola (ed.) (1959) *Trends in Content Analysis*. Urbana, IL: University of Illinois Press.

Radway, J. (1987) *Reading the Romance: Women, Patriarchy, and Popular Literature*. London and New York: Verso.

Saussure, F. de. (1969) *Cours de linguistique générale*. Paris: Payot.

Saussure, F. de. (1983) *Course in General Linguistics*. London: Duckworth.

Saussure, F. de. (1993) *Saussure's Third Course of Lectures on General Linguistics (1910–1911), from the Notebooks of Emile Constantin*. Oxford: Pergamon.

Saussure, F. de. (1996) *Saussure's First Course of Lectures on General Linguistics (1907), from the Notebooks of Albert Reidlinger*. Oxford: Pergamon.

Screen (1992) *The Sexual Subject: A 'Screen' Reader in Sexuality*. London and New York: Routledge.

Shils, E. (1961) 'Mass Society and Its Culture', pp. 1–27 in N. Jacobs (ed.) *Culture for the Millions? Mass Media in Modern Society*. Princeton, NJ: D. Van Nostrand.

Signorielli, N. and Morgan, M. (eds) (1990) *Cultivation Analysis: New Directions in Media Effects Research*. Newbury Park, London and New Delhi: Sage Publications.

Sparks, C. (1996a) 'The Evolution of Cultural Studies . . .', pp. 14–30 in J. Storey (ed.) *What Is Cultural Studies? A Reader*. London: Arnold.

Sparks, C. (1996b) 'Stuart Hall, Cultural Studies and Marxism', pp. 71–101 in D. Morley and K-H. Chen (eds) *Stuart Hall: Critical Dialogues in Cultural Studies*. London: Routledge.

Stone, P. J., Dunphy, D. C., Smith, M. S. and Ogilvie, D. M. (1966) *The General Inquirer: A Computer Approach to Content Analysis*. Cambridge, MA: MIT Press.

Storey, J. (1993) *An Introductory Guide to Cultural Theory and Popular Culture*. New York and London: Harvester Wheatsheaf.

Swingewood, A. (1977) *The Myth of Mass Culture*. London: Macmillan.

Thompson, E. P. (1968) *The Making of the English Working Class*. Harmondsworth: Penguin Books.

Tudor, A. (1979) 'On Alcohol and the Mystique of Media Effects', pp. 6–14 in J. Cook and M. Lewington (eds) *Images of Alcoholism*. London: BFI/AEC.

Tudor, A. (1980) 'Modern Film Theory: Metz's Semiotics', *Australian Journal of Screen Theory*, 8.

Tudor, A. (1982) *Beyond Empiricism: Philosophy of Science in Sociology*. London, Boston, Melbourne and Henley: Routledge & Kegan Paul.

Tudor, A. (1995) 'Culture, Mass Communication and Social Agency', *Theory, Culture & Society*, 12: 81–107.

Turner, G. (1990) *British Cultural Studies*. Boston: Unwin Hyman.

Wellek, R. (1937) 'Literary Criticism and Philosophy', *Scrutiny*, March: 375–383.

Willer, D. and Willer, J. (1973) *Systematic Empiricism: Critique of a Pseudo-Science*. Englewood Cliffs, NJ: Prentice-Hall.

Williams, R. ([1958] 1961) *Culture and Society 1780–1950*. Harmondsworth: Penguin Books.

Williams, R. (1962) *Britain in the Sixties: Communications*. Baltimore, MD: Penguin Books.

Williams, R. ([1961] 1965) *The Long Revolution*. London: Chatto & Windus.

Williams, R. (1989) *Resources of Hope*. London: Verso.

Willis, P. (1977) *Learning to Labour: How Working Class Kids Get Working Class Jobs*. London: Saxon House.

Wollen, P. (1969a) *Signs and Meaning in the Cinema*. London: Secker & Warburg/ British Film Institute.

Wollen, P. (ed.) (1969b) *Working Papers on the Cinema: Sociology and Semiology*. London: British Film Institute.

Wood, R. (1968) *Howard Hawks*. London: Secker & Warburg/British Film Institute.

Wood, R. (1969) *Hitchcock's Films*. London: A. Zwemmer.

Wren-Lewis, J. (1983) 'The Encoding/Decoding Model: Criticisms and Redevelopments for Research on Decoding', *Media, Culture and Society*, 5: 179–197.

Wright, W. (1975) *Sixguns and Society: A Structural Study of the Western*. Berkeley: University of California Press.

Wrong, D. H. (1961) 'The Oversocialised Conception of Man in Modern Sociology', *American Sociological Review*, 26: 183–193.

Index